The Easy

IPHONE 15 FOR SENIORS

Discover iPhone 15 with Ease! A Fully Large Illustrated, Step-by-Step, Non-Tech-Savvy Guide with Clear, User-Friendly Explanations for Seniors and Beginners

SageTech Publishing

Explore exclusive benefits now!

Scan the QR code to claim your bonus and enhance your experience today

Table of Contents

Chapter 1:
Introduction and Getting Started

Welcome and Book Overview

In this comprehensive guide, we aim to provide seniors with an in-depth understanding of the iPhone 15 and its features. As technology continues to evolve, it's important for seniors to stay connected & take advantage of the many benefits that smartphones offer. The iPhone 15, with its advanced capabilities & user-friendly interface, is an excellent choice for seniors looking to embrace the digital age.

Throughout this guide, we will explore the various features of the iPhone 15, tailored specifically to meet the needs and preferences of seniors. We understand that transitioning to a new device can be daunting, but rest assured, we will take you step-by-step through the process, making it easy for you to navigate and enjoy all that the iPhone 15 has to offer.

From basic functions like making calls, sending text messages, and managing contacts, to exploring the App Store, using social media, and accessing your favorite entertainment platforms, we will cover it all. Additionally, we will delve into the accessibility features of the iPhone 15, designed to enhance usability for individuals with visual, auditory, or motor impairments, ensuring that everyone can fully enjoy the device's capabilities.

Whether you're a newcomer to smartphones or have experience with previous iPhone models, this guide will serve as your go-to resource for mastering the iPhone 15. Our aim is to empower you with the knowledge and confidence to utilize your iPhone 15 to its fullest potential, keeping you connected with loved ones, exploring new horizons, and enriching your digital experience.

So, let's embark on this journey together and unlock the endless possibilities of the iPhone 15. Get ready to discover a world of convenience, entertainment, and connectivity right at your fingertips!

Unboxing and Initial Setup

What's Inside the Box?

- iPhone 15
- Braided Type-C to Type-C charging cable
- User manual
- SIM ejector tool
- A couple of Apple stickers

When you open the packaging of any Apple device, you are in for an adventure. The iPhone 15 is not an exception to this rule. First and foremost, the process of unpacking the package is straightforward and uncomplicated. Your next stop will be the iPhone 15 Pro Max, which is positioned from the display side and has a paper protector at the top of the device.

When you remove it, you will see the new braided charging cable that connects Type-C to Type-C. This is the first time that Apple has incorporated a braided cable in their product lineup. Apple stickers, the user handbook, and the SIM ejection tool are the other items included in this package.

To a large extent, that is the only thing we are provided with within the new iPhone 15 Pro Max packaging.

Setting Up Your New iPhone 15

Setting up a new iPhone can be tricky, especially if you're a first-time user and new to the Apple ecosystem. This section will show you how to set up your iPhone from start to finish.

Turn on your iPhone

1. Hold down the Side button 'til you see the Apple logo to turn on your iPhone. When it finishes booting, it launches into a "**Hello**" page, where it displays the "Hello" word in several languages. On the "**Hello**" setup page, swipe up from the screen's bottom to proceed.

Swipe up from the bottom to start the setup

2. Choose your language from the language list.

3. Choose your country of residence.

Please keep in mind that your choice of country influences the appearance of content on your iPhone.

- Go over the **Quick Start** on-screen prompts to transfer your files to your new device. With the "**Quick Start**" feature, your iPhone temporarily downloads all your content into iCloud and then downloads it onto your new iPhone. Apple's Quick Start is secure and without risk of breach. However, if you want to use the device without moving your files onto it, tap "**Set Up Manually**."

Set up your Wi-Fi on New iPhone

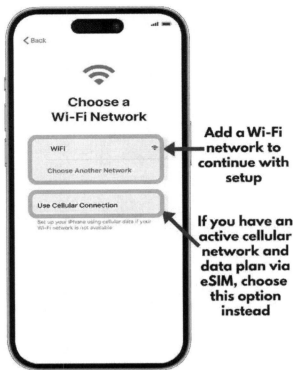

- Select your preferred Wi-Fi network and then follow the on-screen directions to connect. Alternatively, if you're configuring an iPhone with live cellular service, you can choose the "**Use Cellular Connection**" option at the bottom-left corner of the screen.

Set Up the iPhone 15's eSIM

All devices in the iPhone 15 lineup (both the Pro and non-Pro models) don't have provision for a physical SIM card. In its place, Apple uses an inbuilt technology called eSIM. An Esim (which is an acronym for embedded subscriber identification module) depends on a built-in chip which has all the properties of a physical SIM card, except that it is embedded into the device's hardware and supports multiple cell services at once. You can register up to eight numbers at once, but only two can be active at any given time.

- On the "Set Up eSIM" screen, you have two options: Set Up Later in Settings or Transfer from another iPhone.

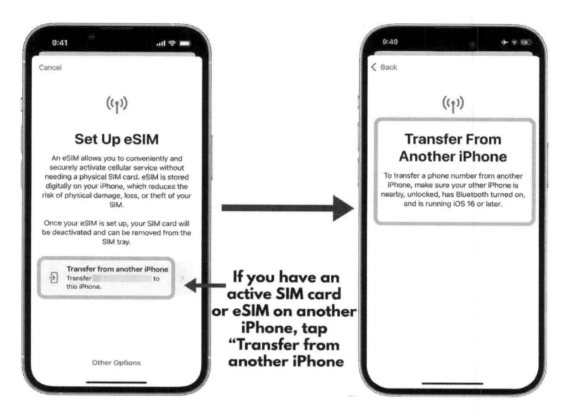

The "Transfer from another iPhone" option allows you to move an operational cellular service from an older iPhone to your new iPhone 15 Pro device. When you choose this option, a pop-up window that says "**Transfer your SIM to this iPhone?**" appears. Then, a warning pops up under this headline, telling you that if you transfer your current phone number and service plan to your new iPhone 15, the network on your old device will stop working. To proceed, select "**Transfer Number**" from the displayed options. You can also choose "**Cancel**" to defer the process until later.

Thereafter, you'll find the "**Setting Up Cellular**" page, notifying you that the eSIM setup process is ongoing. When you're done, you'll see a new page with "Cellular Setup Complete," letting you know that your new iPhone now has an active eSIM cell service.

- Tap "**Continue**" to carry on with the rest of the setup process.

Go over iPhone's Data & Privacy

- Tap "**Continue**" on the "**Data & Privacy**" setup page.

Face ID Setup

- On the Face ID setup page, tap "**Continue**" and then follow the on-screen directions to activate it. You can tap "**Set Up Later in Settings**" if you wish to skip the setup for now.

Set a Passcode

- Input any six-figure passcode of your choosing in the "**Passcode**" setup screen. However, make sure it is one you can easily remember. Next, enter the passcode again.

Log in your Apple ID

- Input your existing Apple ID (if you have one), then tap the "**Next**" button. If you've forgotten the Apple ID or password, use the "**Forgot password**" tab under the Apple ID setup screen. You can also tap the "**don't have an Apple ID**" tab to create a new Apple ID. Next, input your Apple ID password and tap "**Next**" to proceed.

Keep your iPhone Protected and Up to Date

- Go through the "**Keep Your iPhone Up to Date**" page and then tap the "**Continue**" button.
- On the "**Location Services**" setup page, tap "**Enable Location Services**" if you wish to use apps like the Weather app or your iPhone's GPS.

- Study the "**Screen Time**" setup page and then tap "**Continue**" to begin its setup, or you can decline by selecting "**Setup Later in Settings**." The Screen Time feature is a digital wellbeing tool that helps keep track of the amount of time you spend using individual apps on your iPhone and sends you the data regularly so that you can make the necessary adjustments.

- The "**App Analytics**" setup page allows you to decide whether to share app usage data with Apple and third-party developers or not. You can accept by tapping "**Share with App Developers**" or decline by selecting "**Don't Share**."

- For the "**Display Zoom**" setup page, choose the zoom size that best suits you and then tap the "**Continue**" button.

Welcome to iPhone

- The "**Welcome to iPhone**" screen indicates that your iPhone has been fully setup and is ready for use. Swipe up from the bottom of the screen to reveal the Home Screen and begin using your iPhone.

Update Your iOS version

The first thing to do is to make sure your iPhone is updated to the latest version of iOS 17. If it's not, make sure you update it right away to get the best possible iOS experience and device protection. The new iOS 17 has just been released, and it offers tons of new features that are all incredible. Update your iOS version as soon as you can. Check whether you have any pending software updates in your settings section by going to **Settings** > **General** > **Software Update**.

- If there is, tap "**Download and Install**" to begin the updating process. In the course of this book, we'll discuss tons of features that come with iOS 17 as well as the iPhone 15 Pro models.

Understanding Your iPhone: A Visual Guide to Basics

The iPhone 15 is equipped with a thoughtfully arranged set of buttons that facilitate easy access and intuitive operation, especially catering to the needs of seniors. The tactile feedback and user-friendly design of these buttons are particularly appreciated by older users. Let's delve into a closer examination of the key buttons and ports, understanding their functions and how they can be advantageous for seniors:

1. **Side Buttons:** Retaining the classic side buttons, the iPhone 15 incorporates easily accessible volume up and down buttons, along with the sleep/wake (or power) button. Positioned conveniently for comfortable use, these buttons boast a simple and well-defined design, ensuring seniors can effortlessly adjust volume or power their device.

2. **Action Button (Pro Models):** In the iPhone 15 Pro models, the traditional mute switch has been replaced by the versatile Action Button. This programmable button can be customized to perform a variety of tasks, providing users, especially seniors, with a more adaptable and versatile device. Seniors can configure the Action Button to meet their specific needs, whether it involves enabling accessibility features, quickly accessing specific apps, or any other function enhancing their user experience.

3. **Lightning Connector:** Transitioning from the traditional Lightning connector to USB Type-C, the iPhone 15 aligns with industry standards and enhances connectivity options. Seniors can benefit from the versatility of USB Type-C, compatible with a wide array of accessories and offering faster data transfer speeds. This ensures quicker and more efficient connections to other devices and accessories.

4. **SIM Card Tray:** The SIM card tray is strategically located for easy access, allowing users to insert or replace their SIM cards with minimal effort. Seniors, especially those needing to switch SIM cards for travel or other purposes, will find this placement convenient, ensuring they can stay connected without any hassle.

Chapter 2:
Comparing iPhone 15 Models

Differences Between iPhone 15, iPhone 15 Plus, and iPhone 15 Pro

The iPhone 15 series represents a significant shift in line with Apple's three-year redesign strategy, showcasing a refreshed design that stands out from the iPhone 12, iPhone 13, & iPhone 14 series. In addition to the updated aesthetic, the iPhone 15 series boasts notable improvements, with the iPhone 15 Pro models leading the pack in enrichments. Get ready to explore all the details about the iPhone 15 & iPhone 15 Pro series, promising to be among the most impressive iPhones to date.

Models

The iPhone 15 series comprises four models: the iPhone 15 & 15 Plus, iPhone 15 Pro & 15 Pro Max. In contrast to the iPhone 13 generation, there is no iPhone 15 Mini in this lineup. Apple opted to discontinue the iPhone Mini model starting from the iPhone 14 generation.

Price

Except for the iPhone 15 Pro Max, the pricing for the iPhone 15 generation matches that of the iPhone 14 generation at its initial release. The iPhone 15 Pro Max, however, comes with a base storage of 256GB, an upgrade from the 128GB option in the iPhone 14 Pro Max. This enhancement raises the starting price of the base model to $1,199, compared to the $1,099 of its predecessor.

It is essential to keep in mind that the pricing listed here may change based on the carrier you use and any prospective trade-in values that you might be able to take advantage of through the greatest discounts on the iPhone 15 and iPhone 15 Pro.

Here's a breakdown of the iPhone 15 series pricing:

- $799 (128GB), $899 (256GB), $1,099 (512GB) for iPhon 15
- $899 (128GB), $999 (256GB), $1,199 (512GB) for iPhon 15 Plus
- $999 (128GB), $1,099 (256GB), $1,299 (512GB), $1,499 (1TB) for iPhon 15 Pro
- $1,199 (256GB), $1,399 (512GB), $1,599 (1TB) for iPhon 15 Pro Max

Cameras

Apple has implemented significant camera enhancements across the entire lineup of iPhone 15 models. The primary cameras on both the iPhone 15 and iPhone 15 Plus have been upgraded from 12 megapixels (MP) to 48MP. This revamped camera system introduces an optical 2x zoom, achieved by utilizing the central 12MP region of the 48MP sensor, delivering a noteworthy addition to the capabilities of the iPhone 15 and iPhone 15 Plus.

By default, photos captured with the iPhone 15 and iPhone 15 Plus are downscaled from 48MP to 24MP, enhancing detail and clarity. Despite the increase in megapixels, Apple assures that the 24MP photos maintain a "practical file size." However, the exact storage usage compared to 12MP photos remains undisclosed at this time.

The iPhone 15 Pro & iPhone 15 Pro Max also feature a 48MP main camera producing 24MP photos. Additionally, Apple has introduced preset options for popular focal lengths such as 24mm, 28mm, & 35mm, enhancing the photographic capabilities of these devices.

The iPhone 15 Pro is equipped with a standard 3x zoom lens, while the iPhone 15 Pro Max boasts Apple's innovative 5x zoom lens with a 120mm focal length. This new 5x zoom lens adopts a "tetraprism" design, akin to the periscope-style 10x zoom lens found on the Samsung Galaxy S23 Ultra, showcasing Apple's unique approach to advanced zoom technology.

Battery Life

Apple did not delve into details regarding battery life improvements for the iPhone 15 series. No enhancements are claimed across any of the iPhone 15 models, and users can anticipate a battery performance comparable to that of the iPhone 14 generation. The iPhone 14 Plus, in particular, impressed us with its outstanding battery life, still maintaining the top position in our battery test among all phones.

Displays

The iPhone 15 generation maintained its traditional display size, but both the iPhone 15 and iPhone 15 Plus saw enhancements in their screens, featuring a brighter 2000 nits compared to the iPhone 14's 1200-nit display. Here are the display specifications for each model:

- 6.1-inch Super Retina XDR OLED display, 60Hz for iPhone 15
- 6.7-inch Super Retina XDR OLED display, 60Hz for iPhone 15 Plus
- 6.1-inch Super Retina XDR OLED, 120Hz ProMotion, AOD for iPhone 15 Pro
- 6.7-inch Super Retina XDR OLED, 120Hz ProMotion, AOD for iPhone 15 Pro Max

Design

The latest design from Apple features softer contoured edges on all models of the iPhone 15, a departure from the sharper edges found on the iPhone 14. This change is expected to enhance the overall comfort of holding the iPhone 15 generation. The iPhone 15 Pro & iPhone 15 Pro Max now sport a Titanium frame with a brushed metal aesthetic, replacing the shiny polished steel of the iPhone 14. This alteration contributes to a lighter overall weight, with the iPhone 15 Pro weighing in at 6.6 ounces, compared to the 7.27-ounce iPhone 14 Pro, & the iPhone 15 Pro Max at 7.81 ounces, a reduction from the hefty 8.47-ounce iPhone 14 Pro Max.

The iPhone 15 Pro & iPhone 15 Pro Max come with slimmer display bezels, enhancing their overall premium appearance. Additionally, their repairability is improved compared to earlier iPhone Pro models, as the glass back is now more easily removable, potentially reducing repair costs.

Colors

The back glass of the iPhone 15 and iPhone 15 Plus showcases Apple's latest color-infused design, presenting a frosted matte texture in a range of five color choices: blue, pink, yellow, green, and black.

The titanium frame of the iPhone 15 Pro and iPhone 15 Pro Max comes in a range of color choices, comprising natural titanium, blue titanium, white titanium, and black titanium.

Performance

The iPhone 15 and iPhone 15 Plus share the A16 Bionic processor found in the iPhone 14 Pro series, suggesting a performance level akin to last year's premium phones. In contrast, the iPhone 15 Pro and iPhone 15 Pro Max are equipped with Apple's latest A17 Pro processor. According to Apple, the A17 Pro boasts a "10 percent faster" CPU & "20 percent faster" GPU (graphics), although the specific basis for these comparisons remains unclear. Apple has prioritized enhanced graphics and gaming capabilities, leveraging hardware-accelerated ray tracing (a technique for creating notable lighting impacts) facilitated by the A17 Pro processor in the iPhone 15 Pro models.

Action button

In the iPhone 15 Pro & iPhone 15 Pro Max, Apple introduced a novel feature by replacing the well-known iPhone ring/silent switch with a versatile Action button. This customizable button allows users to assign various functions, such as activating the flashlight, swiftly launching apps like Camera, Voice Memos, and Translate, configuring a Focus mode, or executing a Shortcut. Notably, users can still opt for the conventional ring/silent switch if they prefer. Meanwhile, the classic ring/silent switch, unchanged since the inception of the first iPhone, continues to be present on the iPhone 15 and iPhone 15 Plus.

USB-C

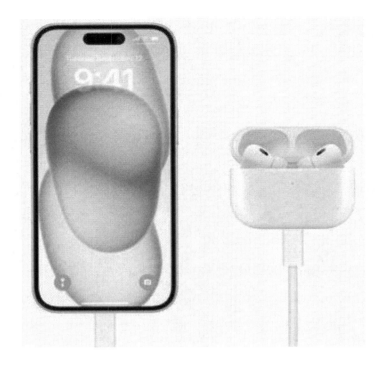

The iPhone 15 series has replaced the Lightning port with a USB-C port across the entire lineup. Despite maintaining the charging speed at 18-20W, consistent with the Lightning port, the new USB-C port enables the charging of other devices using a USB-C cable, such as the latest AirPods Pro 2 with USB-C compatibility.

One thing that should be brought to your attention is the fact that the USB-C ports on the ordinary iPhone 15 models and the iPhone 15 Pro models are quite different from one another. Both the iPhone 15 and the iPhone 15 Plus are the only devices that enable USB 2 transfer speeds, which can frequently approach 480 Mbps. In contrast, the USB-C ports on the iPhone 15 Pro and iPhone 15 Pro Max support USB 3 speeds. The iPhone 15 Pro models can achieve speeds of up to 10Gb/s, indicating compatibility with the USB 3.1 Gen 2 standard.

Dynamic Island

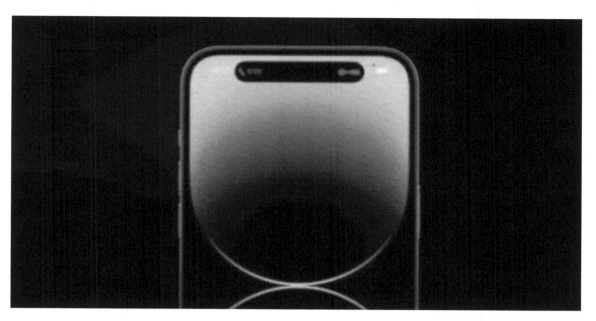

The iPhone 15 and iPhone 15 Plus now feature Apple's Dynamic Island, a design element originally introduced in the iPhone 15 Pro (and iPhone 14 Pro) models. This innovative feature replaces the notch, which was initially informed with the iPhone X in 2017.

Roadside Assistance via satellite

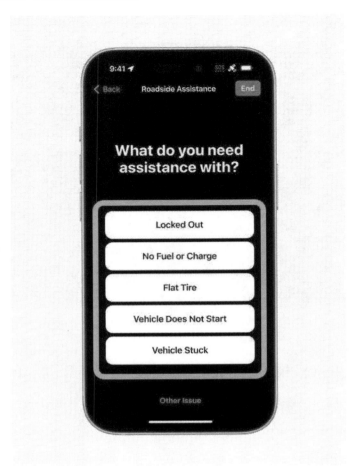

The most recent safety addition from Apple, named Roadside Assistance via satellite, links individuals facing car troubles in locations without WiFi or cellular signal to AAA for assistance. This service is complimentary for the first two years after activating a compatible iPhone and is compatible with AAA memberships. For non-AAA members, it operates on a pay-per-use model.

Introduced with the iPhone 15 generation, Roadside Assistance via satellite is also compatible with the iPhone 14 generation. It enhances the current safety features, such as Crash Detection and Emergency SOS via satellite.

Choosing the Right Model for Your Needs

iPhone 15 Pro Max: Perfect for Photography and Multimedia Aficionados

Tailored for senior users who appreciate superior photography and immersive multimedia experiences, the iPhone 15 Pro Max boasts an upgraded zoom lens for capturing distant subjects with its impressive 5x optical zoom. The device offers an exceptional multimedia experience through its expansive 6.8-inch AMOLED display and dual-channel speakers, making it an optimal choice for enjoying shows and videos. Despite weighing 221 grams, its ergonomic design, featuring thinner bezels and a lighter Titanium material, enhances user comfort.

iPhone 15 Pro: Striking a Balance Between Portability and Power

Designed with a 6.1-inch form factor, the iPhone 15 Pro combines portability with powerful features. Sharing the capabilities of the Pro Max, comprising the A17 Pro Bionic chip and iOS 17 features, it boasts a 48MP primary sensor for high-quality photos and videos. Users can choose between the Pro and Pro Max, with a $200 price difference for the larger device.

iPhone 15 Plus: A Cost-Effective Large-Screen Choice

Priced starting at $899, the iPhone 15 Plus offers a budget-friendly option for those desiring a large-screen iPhone experience. The 6.8-inch panel provides a similar viewing experience to the Pro Max, complete with a Dynamic Island interface. Catering to users who prioritize fundamental features and aesthetics, the 15 Plus is more budget-friendly than its Pro counterparts. Note that its display has a 60Hz refresh rate, and its speakers are not as robust as the Pro Max's.

iPhone 15: An Affordable Yet Feature-Rich Selection

Starting at $799, the standard iPhone 15 often comes with carrier promotions, such as buy-one-get-one or trade-in deals. While lacking some advanced features found in the Pro models, it offers excellent value for its price. Consider the iPhone 15 if features like ProRes video recording, a 120Hz ProMotion display, and an A17 Pro Bionic chip aren't top priorities.

When choosing the right iPhone model as a senior, align your decision with your specific needs, whether it be photography, multimedia, portability, or budget-consciousness. Additionally, the availability of various colors, including pastel options, adds a personal touch to your decision-making process.

Overview of Unique Features in Each Model

The iPhone 15 lineup introduces four distinct models, each boasting unique features to cater to diverse user preferences. Starting with the standard iPhone 15, users can enjoy a vibrant 6.1-inch OLED display with a smooth 60Hz refresh rate, ensuring a visually pleasing experience. Weighing in at 6.02 oz (171 grams), it is the epitome of a balanced and lightweight device. Powered by the A16 Bionic processor and offering 4GB of RAM with storage options ranging from 128GB to 512GB, the iPhone 15 guarantees seamless performance and ample storage capacity.

For those seeking a larger screen, the iPhone 15 Plus steps up with a 6.7-inch OLED display, maintaining the 60Hz refresh rate for a captivating visual experience. Weighing 7.09 oz (201 grams), it offers a substantial feel in hand. Like its counterpart, it shares the A16 Bionic chip and storage configurations, ensuring a consistent and reliable performance across the board. What sets it apart is the extended battery life, providing users with up to 26 hours of video playback.

Moving on to the iPhone 15 Pro, it raises the stakes with a 6.1-inch OLED display boasting an impressive 120Hz refresh rate for smoother interactions. The introduction of the A17 Pro Bionic chip enhances overall processing power, while the 8GB RAM and storage options ranging from 128GB to 1TB ensure users have the capacity for demanding tasks and ample multimedia storage. The camera system is also elevated, featuring a 48MP Wide, 12MP Ultra-wide, and a 12MP 3X Telephoto lens, delivering unparalleled photography versatility.

The flagship of the lineup, the iPhone 15 Pro Max, takes things a step further. Its expansive 6.7-inch OLED display with a 120Hz refresh rate offers an immersive visual experience. Weighing 7.81 oz (221 grams), it provides a substantial yet comfortable feel in hand. The A17 Pro Bionic chip, coupled with 8GB of RAM and storage options ranging from 256GB to 1TB, ensures unparalleled performance and storage capacity. The camera system is a standout feature, boasting a 48MP Wide, 12MP Ultra-wide, and an impressive 5X Telephoto lens for capturing detailed shots from a distance.

All four models share the iOS 17 software, providing a cohesive and intuitive user experience. With IP68 durability, they are resistant to water and dust, offering peace of mind in various environments. The color options vary, allowing users to express their style, with standard hues like Pink, Yellow, Blue, Green, and Black, and the Pro models introducing sophisticated choices such as Natural Titanium, Blue, White, and Black. Connectivity remains cutting-edge with 4G LTE, 5G, eSIM, and satellite capabilities, ensuring a seamless and versatile communication experience. Whether one prioritizes display size, camera capabilities, or overall performance, the iPhone 15 lineup caters to a spectrum of user needs.

Chapter 3:
Mastering Basic Functions

Navigating the Home Screen, Control Center, and Notifications

Navigating the Home Screen and Gestures

You are able to exert control over your gadget by performing particular hand movements.

Opening An App

1. Choose an application to launch. To go back to the home screen, swipe upward from the bottom of the display.

2. Navigate through home screens by swiping left or right. The dots located above the Dock indicate the number of home screens and highlight the one currently in view.

View Or Close a Running App

1. Slide your finger upward from the screen's bottom without lifting it.

2. Navigate through open apps by swiping left or right. Choose the app you want by selecting it.

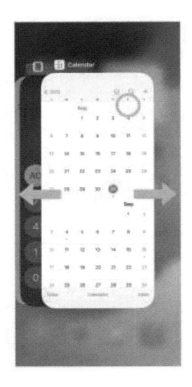

3. To exit an application, choose the desired app and drag it to the top of the screen.

Lock The Screen Orientation

- Swipe down from the top right corner of the screen to open Control Center, then select the Screen Orientation Lock icon. This will allow you to lock the screen in portrait orientation.

View Notifications Or Widgets

- To check your latest Push Notifications, simply swipe down from the top of the screen. Once in the Notifications panel, swipe right to access your widgets.

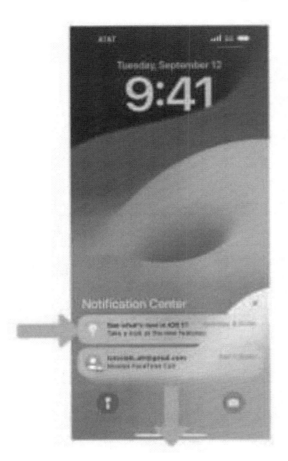 

Move An App

- Tap and hold an app, then choose "Edit Home Screen." Drag the desired app to your preferred location. Once done, tap "Done" to save your arrangement.

Note: You also have the option of tapping and holding an application till it shakes, and then dragging it to the spot you want it to be.

Add Or Remove a Folder

1. When organizing your apps, simply drag one app onto another to form a folder. To change the folder's name, click on the X icon beside the current name, input your preferred folder name, and click done once you're done.

2. To delete a folder, you need only select all of the applications and then drag them outside of the folder. Next, the folder is going to be removed from the system automatically.

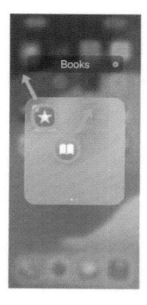

Reset Home Screen Layout

- Navigate to Settings app from home screen, go to General, scroll down to find and choose Transfer or Reset iPhone, then select Reset. After that, opt for Reset Home Screen Layout and confirm the action to reset your home screen.

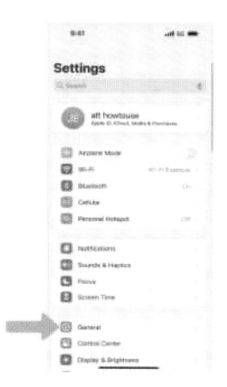

Making and Receiving Calls

The phone application serves the purpose of initiating phone calls. It encompasses various functionalities designed to assist in handling both incoming and outgoing calls, as well as managing voicemail. Accessing the phone app is as simple as clicking its icon located in the Dock at the bottom of the home screen.

What You Need to Know about the Phone App

The diagram below illustrates the features you'll see when you open the phone app.

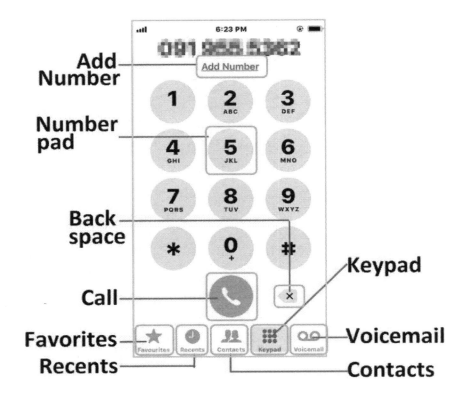

The phone app contains 5 tabs:

1. Voicemail

2. Keypad

3. Contacts

4. Recents

5. Favorites

Keypad: This is used for typing in phone numbers you wish to save to your contacts or give a phone call. When you tap this tab, you'll find the following features:

Number Pad: This is used for typing. Click the numbers on this pad to manually fill in a person's phone number.

Add Number: Type in someone's phone number and click on Add Number. This is going to open a screen where you can choose to either save the number to one of your existing contacts or create a new contact.

Backspace: You can click this key to erase a wrong number which you accidentally typed, one number at a time.

Call Button: After typing in a phone number with the number pad, you can press this button to place a call to that person.

Contacts: Tap Contacts to select a contact you've previously saved. You can view recommended contacts based on your call history.

Recents: Tap Recent to select from those you called recently.

Favorites: Tap Favorites to select from the contacts stored in your favorites.

Making Calls

You have two options for initiating a call using the Phone application. You can either manually input the phone number or choose to call someone from your contacts or favorites list.

To dial a number:

1. Open the phone app by clicking its icon in the Dock at the bottom of the home screen.

2. Click on the keypad tab at the bottom of the screen and enter the phone number you want to call.

3. Click on the green Call to make a call.

4. When the call is over, tap the red End button to close it.

5. In some applications such as Email and Safari, you can call a phone number by simply tapping the number or call button.

To call a contact:

As an alternative of manually dialing the number, you can save the phone number to your phone as a contact. The lessons on adding and managing contacts will go into more detail about contacts.

1. Open the phone app. The list of contacts you've saved will be displayed.

2. Click Contacts 👥 tab at the base of the screen, and then click on the name of the contact you wish to call. If you have a lot of contacts, you can use the row of Alphabets on the right to quickly move to contacts which begin with a particular letter.

3. Click on the desired contact's phone number to make your call.

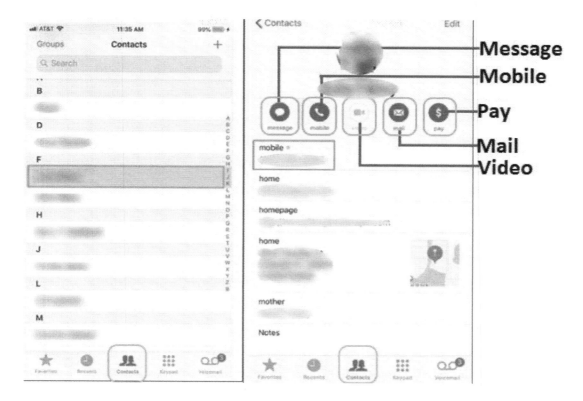

The next screen will contain details of this contact. You can add other details on this screen by tapping Edit at the top right of the screen.

1. To call your friend, click on mobile.

2. When the call ends, tap End⬤ to end it.

Favorite

In the event that you phone the identical contacts on a consistent basis, you can add them to your list of favorites. When compared to picking a contact from the contact list, this may be found to be simpler. Simply launch the **Phone** application, navigate to the **Favorites**★ tab located at the bottom of the screen, and then hit the + button to include an existing contact to your list of favorites. Tap the contact you wish to call in order to make a call to your favorites.

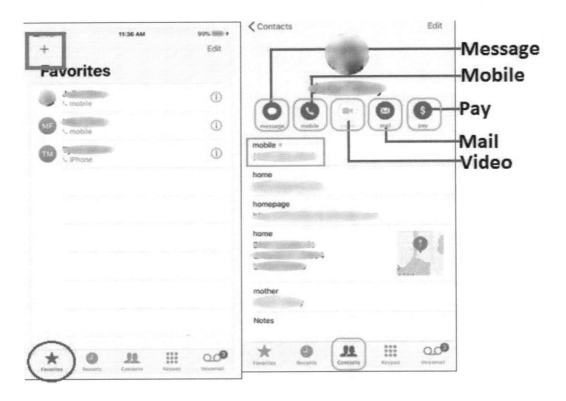

Active call options

Many people enjoy making calls to friends and relatives. It's a way of reaching out, knowing how we're all doing. But the phone app in your iPhone has more to offer than you may instantly realize. For example, while on a phone call, pause and take a good look at your phone's screen. You'll notice that there are several actions you can take during that call. As an illustration, you have the ability to include a second person in your conversation or to transform a voice call into a video call. Let's consider some of these.

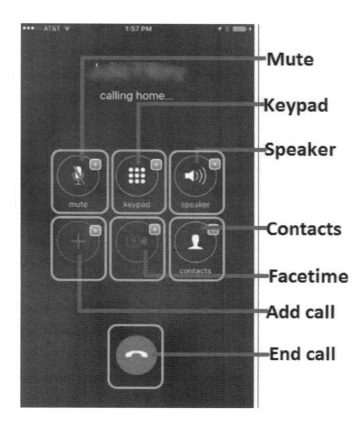

- **Mute** 🔇: Click this button to turn off your microphone temporarily (e.g in a conference call). Click this button a second time if you want to free your microphone to speak.

- **Keypad**: Click on the keypad to open the number pad so that you can type in a number while you're on a call, for example a PIN or another phone number.

- **Speaker**: Click on this button to turn on/off the phone's speaker (for example, while you're on a voice call with several other people present, you can turn on the speaker so that they too can hear).

- **Contacts**: Click on contacts key to access your phone's contacts list.

- **Facetime**: Click on this button to switch your call from Voice call to Video call (available for iPhone to iPhone calls).

Answering and rejecting calls

If your phone is in lock screen mode and you receive a call, you can choose to answer or reject it. Drag the green phone to answer the incoming call. To turn off the ringtone, press the side button. To reject the call then send it directly to voice mail, press the side button twice.

If you're already using your iPhone, click **Accept** to answer the call, or click **Decline** to reject the call.

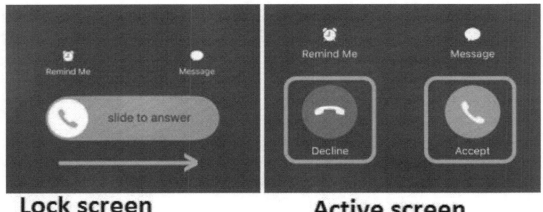

Lock screen   **Active screen**

You can alternatively hit the **Message** button to send a text message in response, or you may click the **Remind Me** button to set a reminder to call that contact at another moment.

Voice mail

Basic voice mail, which enables callers to leave voice messages, is included in virtually all cell service subscriptions. Visual voice mail is also included on the majority of iPhones. This is a function that gives you the ability to view and manage your voicemail messages in a rather straightforward list. The Phone program is very simple to generate and handle greetings and other forms of communication.

To set up visual voice mail:

1. If voicemail isn't already set up, tap the phone icon on your home screen to open the phone app, click on the voicemail tab ⚬⚬ at the bottom right, and select **Set up now**.

2. Use the keypad to enter your voicemail 4-digit password. (Fill it twice to confirm it).

3. Moving further, you are going to have to choose the concluding greeting. The **Default** greeting is the one that gets chosen by default. Select the **Custom** option to customize the greeting.

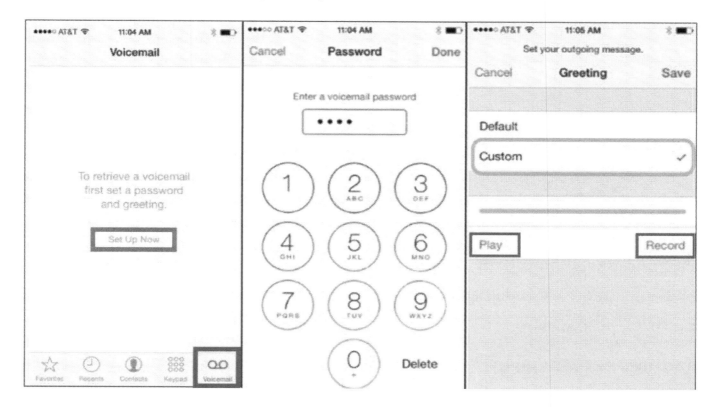

4. Beginning the recording of the greeting, click the **Record** button. If you are finished, hit the **Stop** button, and then tap the **Play** button to preview your message. You can record a fresh greeting by tapping the Register button once more.

5. When you're happy with your greeting message, tap **Save**.

To listen to voice mail:

You can listen to voice messages left by callers whom you missed their calls. When someone leaves a voicemail for you, it's represented by a badge on the voicemail tab. The number on the badge corresponds to the number of voicemails.

1. Tap phone icon on the home screen to open the phone app, and then tap the voice mail tab  at the bottom right.

2. Click the message to listen.

3. To listen to the chosen message once more, touch the play button on your device. You may additionally select the Delete or Callback option.

Sending and Receiving Text Messages and Emails

Text messaging, or SMS (Short Message Service), has become an integral part of our communication in the digital age. Whether you're sending a quick message to a friend or having a more extended conversation, your iPhone 15 makes it easy to send and receive text messages.

Sending Text Messages:

1. **Unlock Your iPhone:** Begin by unlocking your iPhone 15 using Face ID, Touch ID, or your passcode.

2. **Open the Messages App:** Locate the Messages app, which is typically found on your home screen. It's represented by a chat bubble icon. Tap on it to open the app.

3. **Compose a New Message:** In Messages app, tap the pencil icon or "New Message" button (location may vary depending on your iOS version). This action will open a blank message screen.

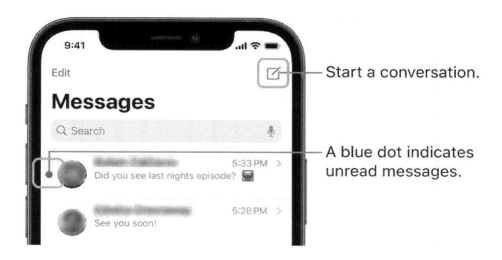

4. **Enter the Recipient:** In the "To:" field, start typing the recipient's name or phone number. As you type, your iPhone will suggest matching contacts from your address book. Tap on the recipient's name or number to select them.

5. **Compose Your Message:** Below the recipient's name, you'll find the message field. Type your message here. You can also add emojis, photos, videos, or other attachments by tapping the relevant icons.

6. **Send the Message:** Once you've composed your message, tap the blue send button (usually represented by a paper airplane icon) to send it. Your message will be delivered to your recipient, and you'll see a confirmation of the sent message.

Receiving Text Messages:

Receiving text messages on your iPhone 15 is just as simple:

1. **Incoming Message Alert:** When you receive a new text message, your iPhone will notify you with a sound, vibration, or on-screen notification, depending on your settings.

2. **Open the Messages App:** To view the incoming message, simply tap the notification banner or open the Messages app from your home screen.

3. **Read and Respond:** Inside the Messages app, you'll see the incoming message. Tap on it to read the full content. To reply, tap the message field at the bottom of the conversation and type your response. Then, tap the send button (paper airplane icon) to send your reply.

Useful Messaging Features:

Your iPhone 15 offers a wide range of features to enhance your messaging experience:

- **iMessage:** iMessage is Apple's instant messaging service that allows you to send text messages, photos, videos, and more to other Apple devices, like iPhones, iPads, and Macs. iMessage is denoted by a blue bubble in the conversation.

- **SMS:** For non-Apple devices or when iMessage is unavailable, your iPhone will send SMS messages, indicated by a green bubble in the conversation.

- **Group Messages:** You can create group messages to chat with multiple friends or family members in one thread. Add multiple recipients when composing a new message.

- **Message Effects:** Add fun and expressive effects to your messages by using features like balloons, confetti, and fireworks. Compose your message, then long-press the send button to access these effects.

- **Digital Touch (iMessage):** With iMessage, you can send digital touches like sketches, heartbeat, or even your heartbeat to your contacts.

- **Memoji and Animoji (iMessage):** Use Memojis and Animojis to create animated characters that mimic your facial expressions and voice. These can be sent as messages and make conversations more playful.

- **Tapbacks:** Respond to messages quickly with tapbacks, which are pre-defined responses like a thumbs-up or heart that you can tap to send in reaction to a message.

- **Message Search:** Easily find specific messages or conversations by using the search bar at the top of the Messages app.

Tips for Better Messaging:

Here are some additional tips to enhance your messaging experience on your iPhone 15:

- **Enable iMessage:** Make sure iMessage is enabled in your device settings to take advantage of its rich messaging features when communicating with other Apple users.
- **Set Up Predictive Text:** Predictive text can speed up your typing. Enable it in the keyboard settings to get word suggestions as you type.
- **Use Siri for Dictation:** Siri can help you compose messages with voice dictation. Simply activate Siri and say, "Send a message to [contact]" followed by your message.
- **Customize Notifications:** Customize your notification settings within the iPhone's settings app to manage the way you receive message alerts and when they are delivered.
- **Delete Messages:** Regularly manage your messages by deleting old conversations or individual messages to free up space on your device.
- **Save Important Messages:** If you have important messages or information, consider using the "Pin" or "Star" feature to keep them easily accessible.
- **Use Quick Replies:** Customize your quick replies in the settings to provide speedy responses to common questions.
- **Secure Messaging:** If you need to send sensitive information, consider using encrypted messaging apps for added security.

- **Turn on Read Receipts:** Enable read receipts if you want your contacts to know when you've read their messages. You can toggle this feature on or off in your message settings.

Regular Software Updates: To ensure you have access to the most recent messaging features, improvements, and security updates, be sure to keep your iPhone's software up to date.

Setting Up and Using FaceTime

FaceTime is a fantastic way to stay connected with loved ones through video calls. It offers a personal touch by allowing you to see and hear the people you care about, even when they're far away. Here's how to set up and use FaceTime:

Enabling FaceTime:

1. To enable FaceTime, go to "Settings" > "FaceTime" and toggle the switch to turn it on. You'll also need an Apple ID to use FaceTime.

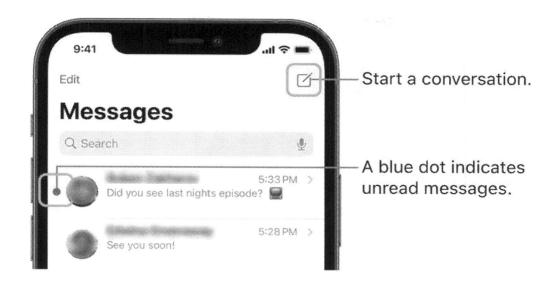

Start a conversation.

A blue dot indicates unread messages.

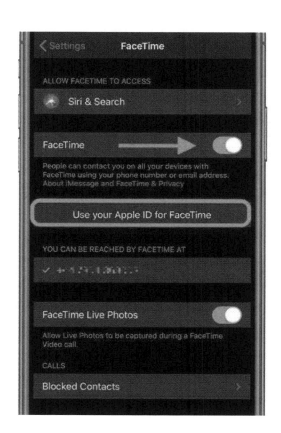

Making a FaceTime Call:

- Open the FaceTime app or go to your Contacts, select a contact, and tap the FaceTime icon to initiate a call. You can also start a FaceTime call during a phone call by tapping the FaceTime icon on the call screen.

Group FaceTime:

- FaceTime allows group calls with multiple participants. To start a group call, tap the "+" icon in the FaceTime app and add the contacts you want to include.

FaceTime Audio:

- You can use FaceTime for audio-only calls. It's a useful feature when you don't want to use video or have limited data connectivity.

FaceTime Effects:

- Make your FaceTime calls more fun by using effects like Animoji and Memojis. These animated characters mimic your expressions and add a playful touch to your calls.

FaceTime for Accessibility:

- FaceTime includes accessibility features like VoiceOver and closed captions, making it user-friendly for those with hearing or vision impairments.

FaceTime has become a cornerstone of modern communication, enabling users to engage in real-time video conversations with family and friends, bridging geographical distances, and providing a sense of connection and presence that text or voice calls alone cannot achieve. Whether you're catching up with a grandchild's latest adventure or sharing a virtual cup of tea with a dear friend, FaceTime is a valuable tool in your iPhone's communication arsenal.

Using The Mail Application

It is highly likely that you will want to establish Mail✉ as one of the initial applications on your iPhone. You are able to use it to manage your inbox, browse and send email, respond to messages, and organize your messages. For the most part, this is the only thing you do with your email account.

Upon opening an email for the first time, sign in to your current email address. Choose your email provider and adhere to the provided instructions to link your account to your email application. After completing these steps, you'll be able to send & receive emails from that account on your iPhone.

Add another email account

You have the ability to add several accounts to your email program if you use different email accounts. For instance, you may have one email account for your personal email and another for your work email. This gives you the ability to keep track of all of your messages in one location.

- To add another email account, open Settings on the home screen and go to **Password & Accounts**> **Add Account**. Simply follow the directions that pop up, to sign in with your new account.

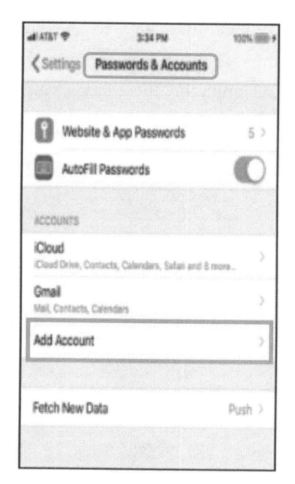

Email notification

To indicate that you have received a new email, a badge will be displayed on the icon of the program. In your inbox, this number indicates the number of emails that have not yet been read. This allows you to quickly check for new messages without having to open the mail application.

- You can customize your alerts by opening Settings, tap Notification Center, and select Email.

Slide gesture

The Mail app contains some useful tools for managing your inbox, such as folders and flags. Swipes can also be used to manage messages in the mail inbox very quickly. For example, you can slide a message to the left if you wish to archive or delete it, reply it, and forward it or something else.

Personalize your email signature

At the bottom of each and every email that you write, the word "sent from iPhone" is automatically included as a default setting. This is the email signature that is used by default as part of your email application. If you want to customize or delete your email signature, open Settings from your home screen, tap Email, then scroll down and select Signature.

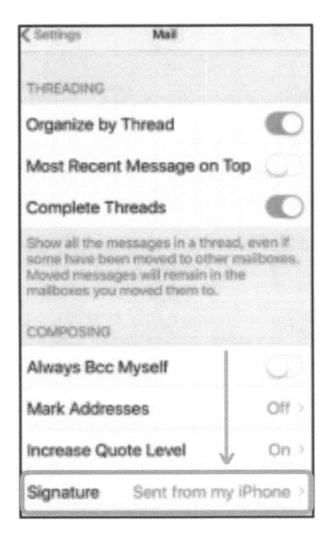

Chapter 4:
Accessibility and Ease of Use

Adjusting Accessibility Settings for Vision and Hearing

The iPhone incorporates numerous features specifically designed to assist individuals facing challenges related to hearing impairment, visual impairment, and various physical limitations. These functionalities can be activated and customized within the Accessibility Settings screen.

Follow these steps to access and configure these features:

1. Open the Settings screen and tap on General.

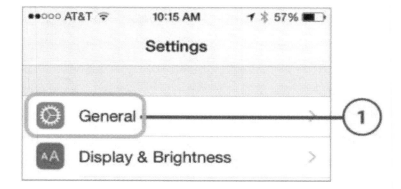

2. Swipe up until you locate the Accessibility option.

3. Tap on Accessibility, where the screen is categorized into sections addressing different limitations. The initial section, VISION, offers options to aid visually impaired users.

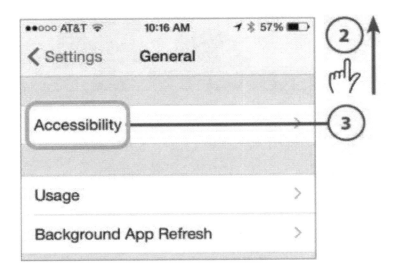

4. Utilize the controls within the VISION section to modify the appearance of the iPhone's screens. Options include:

- **VoiceOver:** Guides through screens by vocalizing their contents.
- **Zoom:** Magnifies the entire screen.
- **Invert Colors:** Alters the screen from dark characters on a light background to the reverse.
- **Grayscale:** Switches to grayscale instead of color.
- **Speech:** Allows the iPhone to speak selected text, screen content, and auto-corrections.
- **Larger and Bold Text:** Increases text size and adds bold, complementing Text Size and Bold settings.
- **Other options:** Adjust button shapes, contrast, motion, and label visibility.

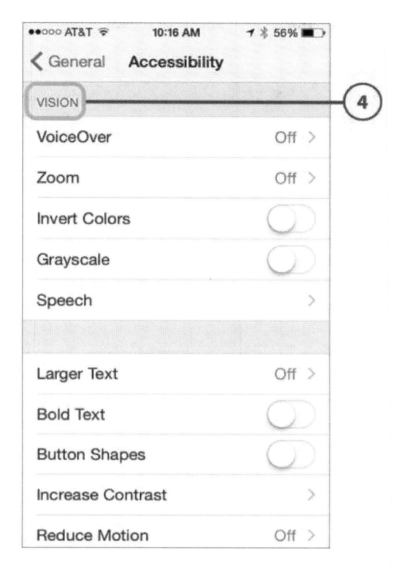

5. Swipe up to access the HEARING section.

6. Use the controls in this section to configure sounds and accommodate hearing-impaired users. Controls include:

- **Hearing Aids:** Pairing with Bluetooth-capable hearing aids.
- **LED Flash for Alerts:** Flashing alerts with visual cues.
- **Mono Audio:** Switching to mono sound output.
- **Phone Noise Cancellation:** Reducing ambient noise during phone calls.
- **Balance:** Adjusting stereo sound balance.

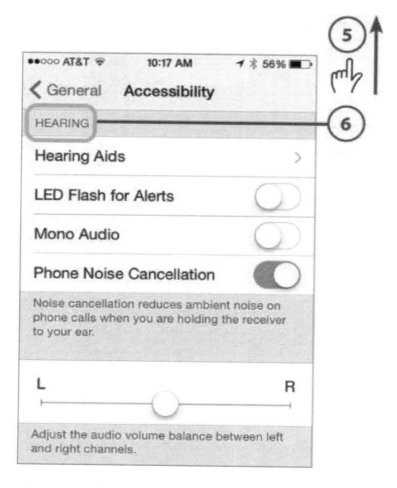

7. Swipe up to navigate to the MEDIA section.

8. Use the controls in this section to enhance video playback features, including:

- **Subtitles & Captioning:** Enabling subtitles and captions with customizable styles.

- **Video Descriptions:** Providing video descriptions when available.

9. Employ the Guided Access setting to restrict the iPhone to a single app and further customize features like Passcode Settings and Time Limits.

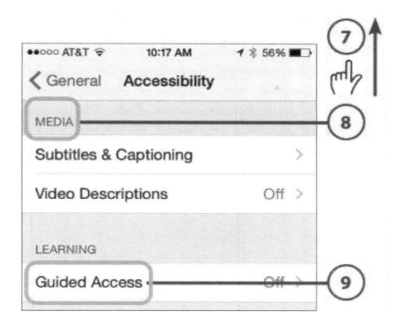

10.   Swipe up to view the INTERACTION section.

11. Adjust how users interact with the iPhone using controls such as:

- **Switch Control:** Configuring the iPhone for adaptive devices.
- **Assistive-Touch:** Simplifying iPhone manipulation with an on-screen button.
- **Call Audio Routing:** Configuring audio output during calls or FaceTime sessions.
- **Home-click Speed:** Adjusting the speed required for Touch ID/Home button double- or triple-press.

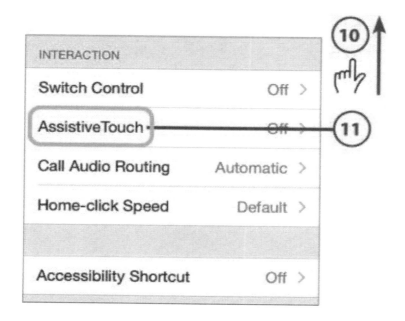

12. Utilize the Accessibility Shortcut control to define the actions triggered when the Touch ID/Home button is pressed three times.

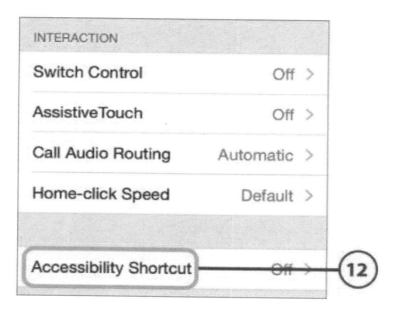

Enlarging Text, Icons, and Using VoiceOver

Changing Text Size

1. Open Settings app by tapping the Settings icon on your Home screen. Scroll down and select Accessibility.

2. Within the Accessibility menu, choose Display and Text Size.

3. Navigate to the Display and Text Size screen and select Larger Text.

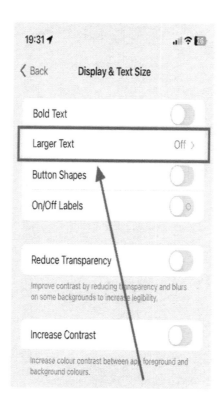

4. Modify the text size by adjusting the slider located at the bottom of the Larger Text Size screen.

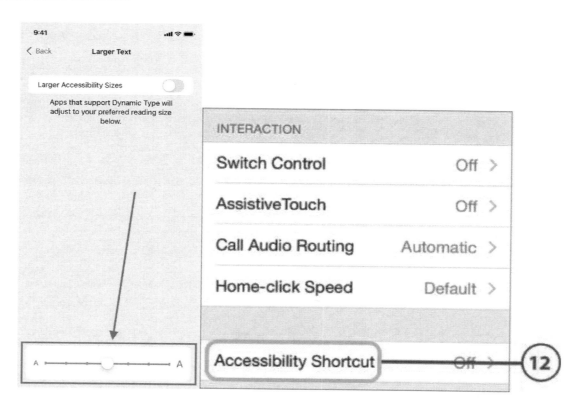

5. For an even larger text size, activate the toggle switch for Large Accessibility Sizes, and then further adjust the slider to your preference.

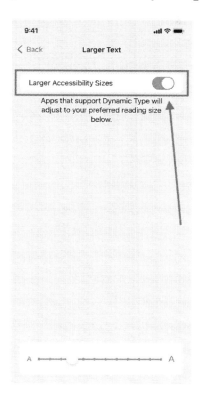

6. When you feel pleased with the settings, you can go back to the Home screen by either swiping up from the bottom of the screen or hitting the Home button (for devices that have a physical Home button).

Adjusting Icon Size

1. Open Settings app on your iPhone 15.

2. Select the Display & Brightness option.

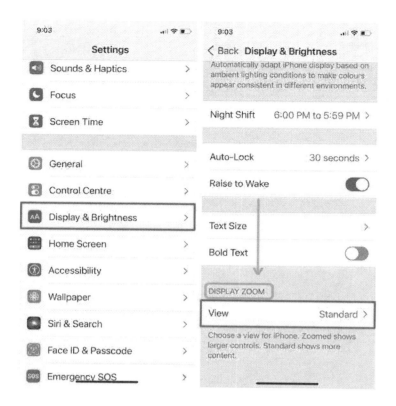

3. Scroll down then tap on View (Display Zoom).

4. Choose between "Standard" or "Zoomed."

5. Tap on Set, and your iPhone will reflect the changes after rebooting once.

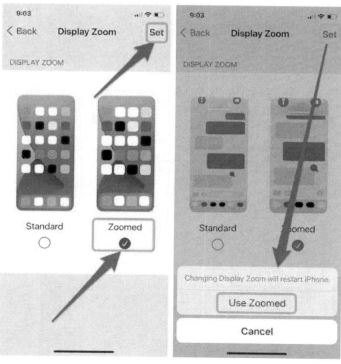

Simplifying Your iPhone Interface

Transforming your new iPhone into a more user-friendly device for seniors doesn't involve a magical button, but certain features can be activated to enhance its accessibility.

Adjust brightness and contrast for better visibility

To modify brightness:

1. Open the Settings app.

2. Select Display & Brightness.

3. Slide the brightness slider to the right.

For contrast adjustments:

1. Access the Settings app.

2. Tap on Accessibility.

3. Choose Display & Text Size.

4. Toggle the Increase Contrast option.

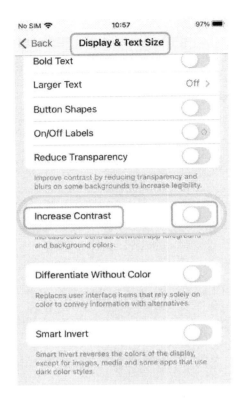

Activate Zoom

In certain instances, your elderly relative or friend might find it beneficial to zoom in on content while using their iPhone. To accomplish this, they can utilize the built-in accessibility feature called Zoom, distinct from the Zoom meeting app.

To enable Zoom:

1. Open the Settings app.

2. Navigate to Accessibility.

3. Select Zoom.

4. Toggle the Zoom switch to activate.

Include Magnifier in the iPhone's Control Center

For enhanced usability tailored to your elderly friend or relative, consider adding the Magnifier button to the iPhone's Control Center. The Magnifier feature transforms the iPhone into a magnifying glass, utilizing the device's rear cameras, which proves particularly useful for reading fine print in newspapers.

To add Magnifier to the iPhone's Control Center:

1. Launch the Settings app.

2. Access Control Center.

3. Scroll down and tap the "+" button next to Magnifier.

To open Magnifier, simply swipe down from the top-right corner of the screen or swipe up from the bottom edge and tap the magnifying glass icon.

Activate the Spoken Content Feature

To enhance the iPhone experience for elderly users, consider enabling the Spoken Content feature, which audibly reads the content displayed on the screen. This feature proves beneficial for individuals with visual impairments and is particularly valuable for those who wish to navigate the internet and consume written content, like Wikipedia articles, without reading it themselves.

Follow these steps to activate Spoken Content:

1. Locate and tap the "Settings" icon on the iPhone's home screen.

2. Select "Accessibility."

3. Choose "Spoken Content."

4. Toggle "Speak Screen" to enable the feature.

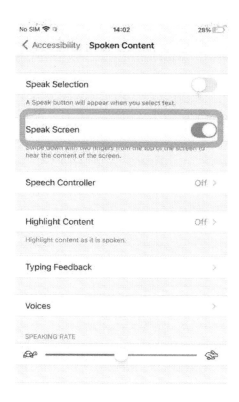

Utilizing the slider located at the bottom of the same screen, you are also able to modify the rate at which you talk. After this update, the iPhone will now read out loud everything that is displayed on the screen whenever the user swipes down with two fingers from the top of the display. You should make sure that you inform the user on how to do this gesture, and if necessary, you should also include written instructions. When it comes to reading text messages, web sites, and news articles, this capability is quite helpful.

Increase iPhone Ring Volume

For an iPhone tailored to seniors, it's essential to have a louder ringtone to accommodate those with hearing impairments.

To amplify the iPhone's ring volume:

1. Find and tap the "Settings" icon on the iPhone's home screen.

2. Select "Sounds & Haptics."

3. Adjust the slider under "Ringtone and Alert Volume" to the right.

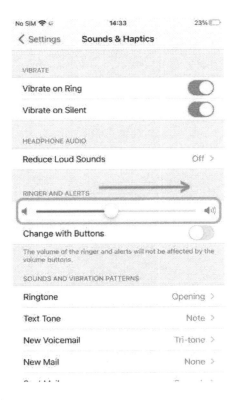

Moving the slider to the right increases the volume of the phone's ringtone. Additionally, in the Sounds and Haptic Patterns section, you can choose a louder ringtone from the Ringtone options.

Configure Hearing Aids

To make iPhones more senior-friendly, they can be paired with Made for iPhone (MFi) hearing aids, third-party devices that support Apple's MFi technology for seamless connectivity.

To pair your elderly relative's MFi hearing device with their iPhone:

1. Make sure that Bluetooth is enabled on your iPhone.

2. Open the battery doors of the hearing device.

3. Access the Settings app on the iPhone.

4. Tap "Accessibility."

5. Select "Hearing Devices."

6. Close the battery doors on hearing device.

7. Once the device name appears under the MFi Hearing Devices section, tap the name.

The pairing process typically takes around 60 seconds. Apple emphasizes that the device should not be used until the pairing is complete. When finished, a sequence of beeps and a tone will indicate successful pairing, and a checkmark will appear next to the hearing device in the Devices list.

Chapter 5:

Communication and Social Media

Managing Contacts and Making Video Calls

Add and manage contacts

With iPhone, you can save your phone number and contact information to your acquaintances. Saved contact information can be used for making quick calls and sending emails. When you have an iPhone, you have the ability to make as many contacts as you require, ensuring that you always have access to vital contact information.

To add a contact:

iPhone has different ways to save contact information from the Phone application.

1. Tap the Contacts tab 👥, then tap the + button in the upper right corner.

2. Press the keypad, type in the phone number, and tap **Add Number**.

Add contact information

When you create a contact, you need to enter the 1st (at least) name, last name, and phone number. However, you can also enter other information such as your email address, address, and birthday.

You can add contact information when you first create a contact, or by opening an existing contact and tapping **Edit**.

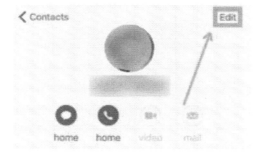

Edit the contact information as needed. When you're done, tap **Done**.

Contact navigation

If you have multiple people stored in your contact list, trying to locate your contacts in a timely manner might be challenging. The good news is that there are two insanely simple methods to get through your contacts account.

- **Search:** The search box that is located at the very top of your contact list allows you to do a rapid search for every one of your contacts. Simply type in the search bar after tapping it. The contacts that match your search are displayed.

- **Browse by text:** Quickly browse your contact list by text. Simply click on the chosen letter on the right side of your list of contacts. You can also swipe up or down to quickly scroll through your contacts.

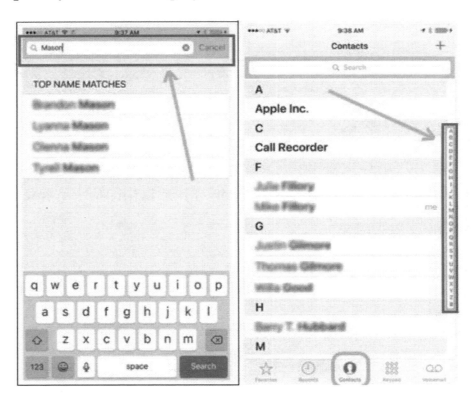

Making Videocall Using Facetime

FaceTime enables you to initiate video calls with individuals listed in your iPhone contacts. Anyone in your contacts possessing FaceTime capability can be contacted through the app. When engaged in a video call, the recipient's face occupies the entire screen, while a smaller screen displays your own image, providing a visual reference for the person you are calling.

In contrast to other video calling applications, FaceTime doesn't maintain a separate contacts list. Instead, it utilizes the existing phone and email contacts list on your phone, tablet, or computer. For instance, if you have a list of contacts on your iPhone for making phone calls, FaceTime automatically identifies which individuals on that list have FaceTime. If any of them have FaceTime, you can easily initiate a call.

To make a FaceTime call on your iPhone, follow these steps:

1. Open the FaceTime app by tapping its icon on the Home screen.

2. Using the on-screen keyboard, choose the Search bar and then type the name of the person you want to call into the search box. FaceTime will look through your contact list to find the name you have chosen.

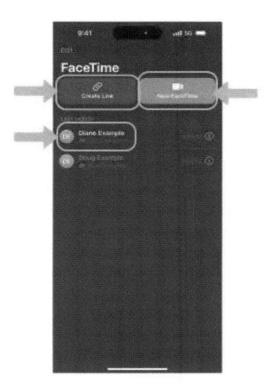

3. If the individual is in possession of FaceTime, a sign of a video camera will show up next to their name. In order to initiate the video call, tap it.

4. The recipient's device will ring, and they can answer the call by tapping the green button.

5. Similar to most video calling apps, FaceTime displays the recipient in full screen, with your image in a smaller window on the screen.

6. To end the call, tap the red end call button when you're ready.

7. During the call, you can mute your microphone by tapping the microphone button. Tap it again to unmute.

8. You can also disable your camera's video by pressing the Home button, taking you to the Home screen. Tap the "Touch to resume FaceTime" bar on the screen to return to the call.

Introduction to Social Media: Staying Connected Safely

Social media has become an integral part of our lives, allowing us to connect and interact with friends, family, and communities online. If you're using an iPhone, you have access to a wide range of social media apps that can enhance your social experiences. Here's a brief introduction to social media and some popular apps that are applicable for seniors:

1. **Facebook:** This is one of the most popular social media platforms worldwide. It allows you to connect with friends and family, share updates, photos, and videos, join groups, and follow pages of your interest. It's a great platform for staying connected with loved ones and discovering new communities.

2. **YouTube:** This is a video-sharing platform where you can watch and upload videos. It offers a wide range of content, including educational videos, tutorials, music, entertainment, and much more. You can create playlists, subscribe to channels, and engage with the YouTube community.

3. **WhatsApp:** A messaging application known as WhatsApp enables users to send and receive text messages, make audio and video conversations, and share photographs and videos with one another. It's widely used for personal communication and has features like group chats, voice messages, and end-to-end encryption for privacy.

4. **Instagram:** Instagram is a platform focused on sharing photos and videos. It allows you to capture and edit pictures, apply filters, and share them with your followers. You can also follow other users, like and comment on their posts, and use Instagram Stories to share moments from your day.

5. **Twitter:** This is a microblogging platform where you can post short messages called tweets. It's known for its real-time updates and is a great platform for sharing thoughts, following news and trends, and engaging in conversations with others.

6. **Pinterest:** Pinterest is a visual discovery platform where you can find and save ideas. It's an excellent platform for discovering and collecting inspiration on various topics like cooking, fashion, home decor, and more. You can create boards to organize your pins and follow other users with similar interests.

7. **LinkedIn:** This is a professional networking platform that lets you to create a professional profile, connect with colleagues, and search for job opportunities. It's useful for building professional relationships, staying updated on industry news, and sharing your expertise.

Ways to Stay Safe on Social Media

Utilizing social media platforms like Facebook, Twitter, and Instagram is a convenient way to stay connected with friends and family. However, it's essential to be mindful of cyber-scammers and identity thieves operating on these platforms. Follow these guidelines to safeguard yourself:

1. **Secure Privacy Settings:** Review the privacy settings on your social accounts to ensure your phone number and email addresses are not publicly visible. Tailor settings based on the platform:

   o On Facebook, adjust privacy settings to restrict post visibility to friends or friends of friends, rather than making them public.

   o In Twitter's safety and security controls, disable "Discoverability" options to prevent searches using your email address and phone number. If using Twitter for private communication, consider enabling the "Protect your tweets" option.

   o For Instagram, set your account to private if you're sharing personal images rather than promoting a business.

2. **Utilize Text Messaging for Security:** While it was once advised to exclude your phone number from social profiles, reconsider this decision. Provide your smartphone number to each platform and enable text messaging for identity confirmation when logging in on a new device. This two-factor authentication or login verification adds an extra layer of security:

   o Enable two-factor authentication on Facebook and customize security settings, including alerts for unrecognized logins.

   o Activate login verification on Twitter.

   o Implement two-factor authentication on Instagram.

3. **Exercise Caution with Location Information:** Avoid sharing your street address to prevent becoming a target for theft. Be discreet about announcing extended travel plans, as an unoccupied home may attract unwanted attention. Prevent inadvertent disclosure of location information by following these steps:

   o On Twitter, disable location tagging by unchecking the "Tweet with location" box in the "Privacy and safety" settings.

- For Facebook and Instagram mobile apps, access your phone's settings, locate location services, and disable them specifically for the Facebook and Instagram apps.

4. **Avoid (and Report) Duplicate Friend Requests:** When you receive a friend request from someone you thought was already in your network, take a moment to double-check your friends list before accepting. If the person is already connected, there's a chance their account has been compromised. Scammers create fake accounts using real users' information to gather friends, relying on mutual connections to expand their deceptive networks. Be cautious, as these fake accounts may use your friend's photos to deceive you. On platforms like Facebook, utilize the reporting feature to notify the friend being impersonated.

   - **For Facebook:** Use the reporting feature for impostors, which automatically notifies the friend being impersonated.
   - **For Twitter and Instagram:** Impersonated individuals must report fake accounts themselves, so reach out to your followers to inform them of any misrepresentation.

5. **Don't Use Social Credentials for Third-Party Sites:** While it might be convenient to register on third-party websites using your Facebook, Google, or Twitter credentials, exercise caution. By opting for this method, you might inadvertently provide more information than necessary. If someone gains access to your social login details, they could potentially infiltrate these third-party accounts as well.

   - **For Facebook:** Review and manage automatically logged-in sites under "Apps" in the Settings page. Disable integration with individual apps or turn off all integration with third-party sites through a single setting.

6. **Avoid Quizzes and Games Requesting Profile Access:** Be wary of quizzes promising to reveal your perfect match, assemble a team, or test loyalty. These seemingly fun activities may actually be schemes to gather your information. Even if they claim not to post without permission, they can harvest your profile info and friends for spamming purposes.

7. **Handle Passwords Securely:** Refrain from storing passwords in your browser to prevent unauthorized access if your device is lost or stolen. Consider password protecting your computer. Change your social media passwords promptly if there's a potential data breach or if your information is on the dark web. Use unique, strong passwords for each account, and consider using a reliable password manager like Dashlane for enhanced security.

8. **Consider Identity Theft Protection:** If you're concerned about potential data compromise, explore identity theft protection products that can alert you to instances of abuse and provide an additional layer of security.

Sharing Photos and Experiences with Family

Discover unique features that allow you and your family to easily share buys, stay in touch, and keep your information safe. If you have kids, you can also control how they use their Apple gadgets.

Set up Family Sharing

Make your Apple experience a family affair by setting up Family Sharing. This feature allows you and your family members to share purchases, subscriptions, locations, and more. Each person maintains their individual device and Apple ID, but things like iCloud storage, subscriptions (such as Apple Music and Apple Arcade), and other content are shared.

To kick off Family Sharing, follow these simple steps:

1. Open Settings on your device.

2. Tap on [your name].

3. Select "Family Sharing."

Share your location with Find My

When you activate Family Sharing, you can let your family members know where you are and assist them in locating misplaced devices using the Find My app.

To share your location with family, follow these steps:

1. Go to Settings > [your name] > Family Sharing.

2. Scroll down and select Location.

3. Tap the name of the family member you want to share your location with.

Once you've shared your location with your Family Sharing group, they can help track down a lost device.

Share Your Health Data

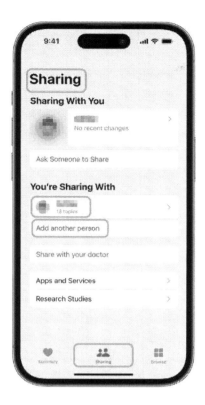

Share your health information easily using the Health app. This includes details about your activity, movement, and health trends, which you can share with your family.

Here's how:

1. Open the Health app.

2. Tap "Sharing" at the bottom of screen.

3. Then, select "Share with Someone."

4. Choose the specific health data you want to share.

5. Decide if you want the recipients to be notified about important trends, like a significant decrease in activity.

Start A Family Photo Library

Create a shared photo library for your family using iCloud. This lets you to share photos and videos with up to five family members. Everyone can contribute by adding, editing, and captioning photos. Plus, you can all relive the memories through shared photos in the memories section, featured photos, and the Photos widget.

Here's how to start:

1. Go to Settings > [your name] > iCloud > Photos.

2. Turn on "Sync this iPhone."

3. Tap "Shared Library" to set up your family photo sharing space.

Add Recovery Contacts

Plan for the unexpected by adding trusted individuals, like family members, as Account Recovery Contacts. This ensures you can regain access to your account if you ever find yourself locked out. Additionally, with the Digital Legacy program, you can designate Legacy Contacts who will have access to your account and personal information in the unfortunate event of your passing.

To add these contacts:

1. Navigate to Settings > [your name] > Sign-In & Security.

2. Choose either "Account Recovery" or "Legacy Contact" based on your preference.

Chapter 6:
Photos, Camera, and Entertainment

Taking and Editing Photos and Videos

Y ou can take pictures with the camera app for iPhone and iPad. You can also take flash photos, high power photos, photo shoots and Selfies. You can also use the volume key or the bottom mode to turn on the remote control.

How to Take a Picture
Using the Shutter icon

1. Open the camera app.

2. Press the shutter icon to capture an image, and it will be stored in the Camera Roll or All Photos Album. You can view it anytime by launching the Photos app.

3. If you'll like to edit it immediately, click the thumbnail preview to view and edit the photo.

How to take a picture with the volume key

If you'll like to use a hard button as your shutter, the volume keys are going to be a good starting point. All you need to do is press!

1. Open the camera app and aim your shot at the object you plan to snap

2. To activate the camera shutter & take a picture, press the volume-up key.

How to take a picture with your headset remote

Many headphones now have controls such as volume keys, which can also be used to turn on the camera shutter. If your headset has a long cable or is wireless headset, you can use it to turn on the camera shutter from long distances.

1. Open your phone's camera app. As usual, aim your shot at the object you plan to snap.

2. Click the hardware volume key in the headset to activate the camera shutter & take a picture.

"Burst mode": How to Snap and Choose Images

A burst is made of many pictures taken rapidly. It's ideal for subjects which are moving rapidly and unevenly (e.g. a bird, a football player on field, etc.)

1. Open the camera app. As usual, aim your shot at the subject you plan to snap.

2. Press then hold the shutter button to capture the image in Burst mode.

3. On iPads, iPhone 11 and iPhone 11 Pro or a newer iPhone model, you can quickly capture the burst mode by pressing and swiping left.

iOS 17 will select the image that it considers to be the best image. If you do not want its choice, you can choose by yourself. After capturing the burst capture, click on the thumbnail preview in the lower left corner.

1. Click the Burst Mode pile you wish to view.

2. Click on **Select**...

3. Now tap the images you want to keep. A blue check marzk will appear beside images you choose.

4. A grayish dot thumb appears below the blue scrub, increasing the focus and position of the image.

5. Tap **Done** to decide what to hold.

If you want to retain all the pictures, tap **Keep Everything**. Click on **Keep Only Favorites** to retain only the ones you pick.

1. Selected images are then taken together in a group and displayed in the camera roll.

How to Activate Flash on iPhone or iPad

1. Open the camera app.

2. Click the Flash icon ⚡ at the upper end.

3. Choose whether to turn it on, off or Auto. On iPads, iPhone 11 or iPhone 11 Pro or a newer model, you need to press the up arrow to see the automatic, on and off options.

Note that in newer iPhone models, when the flash is turned **On** or is on **Auto**, Night Mode will not come on. It will use the flash instead.

How to Set a Timer for iPhone Camera

1. Open the camera app.

2. Tap arrow at the top of the screen or swipe the shutter button upward.

3. Tap the timer icon⏱.

4. Select a 3-second or 10-second time.

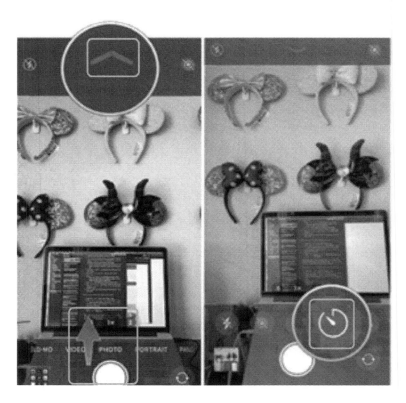

5. Tap the camera shutter-release button to start counting.

While the counter is reading, your iPhone's screen flashes. Numeric numbers are also displayed on the screen and the device provides a vibratory response (if present) when the image is taken.

How to Shoot a Selfie

1. Open the camera app.

2. Tap the Flip Camera ↻ icon to switch between the front camera and the rear cameras.

3. Tap the shutter-release button to take a photo or start a video.

How to Take a Square Photo

1. Open the camera app.

2. Tap arrow at the top of the screen, and/or swipe across the shooting modes till you get to **Square**.

3. Click the shutter icon to shoot your square picture.

How to Take a Panorama

1. Open the camera app.

2. Swipe across the shooting modes till you get to **Pano**.

3. A straight yellow line will appear across the camera screen. You'll also see a white arrow pointing in one direction on the line.

4. If necessary, tap the arrow keys to change the shooting direction.

5. Tap the shutter key ⬤ to start shooting a panorama.

6. Move your iPhone constantly (rotate or pan) in the direction of the arrow while the panorama is being taken to capture as much as you want in your environment. Try aligning the point of the white arrow with the yellow line.

7. Press the shutter button again to complete the panorama.

The camera application does not currently support full 360 degree panorama. Please note that you can take a panorama up to 240 degrees with a single image. Most times you won't use up to 240°.

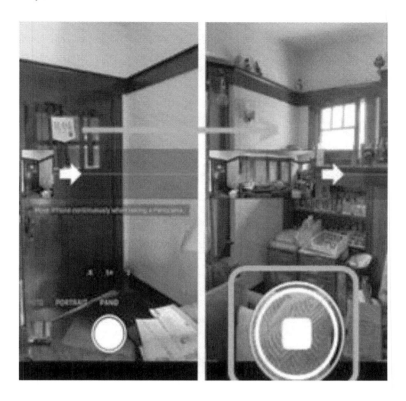

How to Use a Live Photo Filter While Shooting a Picture

1. Open the Camera app

2. Tap arrow at the top of the screen or swipe upward from above the image area of the screen (the viewfinder)/the shutter button.

3. You can also click on the Live Photo filter icon at the top left of the screen. This looks three circles spread out within each other.

4. Select the filter you want to use. Examples include Vivid, Dramatic, etc.

5. Click the shutter button. Your image will be taken.

Edit a Live Photo

You can mute sounds in a live photo, trim the length or change the main photo.

1. Press the ◎icon to make the following changes:

2. To choose one primary photo from the lots, move the white frame to the photo you want, & then press **Make Key Photo** & press **Done.**

3. To trim the photo length, drag one end of the frame viewer to select the frames for the Live Photo.

4. To turn the Live Photo into a still photo, press **Live** at the top of the screen. You would only see the key photo. Press Live again to undo.

5. Tap ◀))at the top of your screen to mute or unmute the photo.

6. Open the Live Photo in the Photos app & press **Edit.**

Edit Photos & Videos

You can rotate, crop, add a filter, add color, & more to your photos & videos.

1. Open the photo or video you want to edit, & press **Edit.**

2. To adjust color & light, swipe under the photo to view the different effects, then click an effect to edit & use the slider to get the desired look.

3. To crop, flip or rotate, press ⌗ & then manually use the rectangle corners to choose the areas you want to retain or tap ▭ to crop to a standard pre-set ratio on the iPhone 15

   o Press ◧ to rotate a picture 90 degrees.
   o Press ⤢ to horizontally flip the picture.

4. Press ● to automatically add effects to your videos or photos.

5. To apply a filter, press ⊛, select the filter, & use the slider to modify the effect.

6. To write or draw on the photo, press Ⓐ & use the different colors & drawing tools to annotate your photo. Press ✛ to add text, captions, your signatures, or shapes.

7. Once you are satisfied with all the edits, press **Done.** Otherwise, press **Cancel** & select **Discard Changes.**

Revert an Edited Photo or Video

To return an edited photo or video to its original copy,

1. Open the photo or video & click **Edit.**

2. Select **Revert** & click **Revert to Original.**

Trim Video Length

Shorten the length of a video with the steps below:

1. Open the video & click **Edit.**

2. Drag one end of the frame viewer to change the stop or start times of the video.

3. Press **Done** & press **Save Video** to keep only the trimmed video, or press **Save Video as New Clip** to have both untrimmed & trimmed videos.

Turn Off the Cinematic effect in a Video

1. Open a video you shot in the Cinematic mode & press **Edit.**

2. Press **Cinematic** at the top of your screen & press **Done.** Do the same thing to return the cinematic effect.

Organizing Your Photo Library

Your photos are organized into different sections that you will find at the bottom of the Photo app screen.

1. Click on each tab to view its content.
2. Click on a photo to open it or a video to play it. Press & hold a Live Photo (has the icon) to play it.
3. Press on the video or photo full screen view to view more details about the photo, like the date & time the photo was taken, the people in the photo, the location the photo was taken, & more.
4. Tap to return to the album.

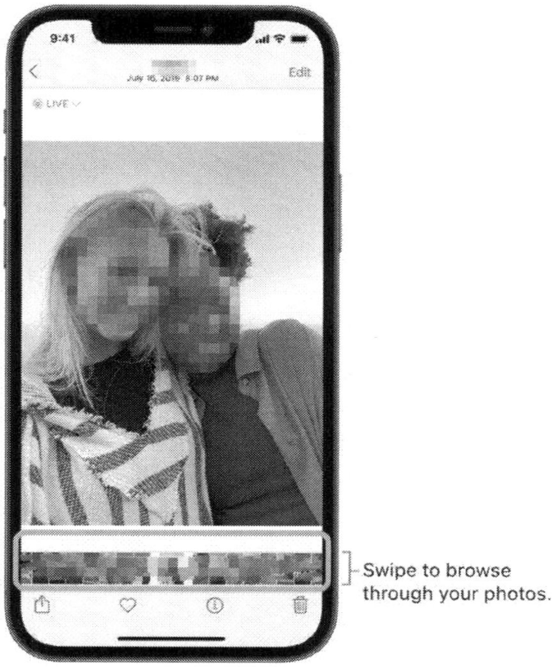
9:41
Edit
LIVE
Swipe to browse
through your photos.

Delete or Hide Video or Photos

1. Open the video or photo & press the icon to delete the content from your phone.
2. Press the icon to hide the content. The hidden content will only appear in the Hidden album.

You can also hide the hidden album with the steps below:

1. In Settings app on your iPhone , click **Photo.**

2. Then switch off the **Hidden Album** button. Turn on the switch to see the album again.

Play a Video

1. Click the video to play it. Then use the player controls at the bottom of the screen to delete, share, favorite, pause, mute, or see more details about the video.

2. Double press your screen to change from full screen to fit-to-screen.

3. Press & hold the frame viewer above the player controls to pause the video, then move the viewer slide right or left to fast-forward or rewind the video.

Permanently Delete or Recover Deleted Photos & Videos

You can recover your deleted photos or choose to permanently delete them off your device.

1. Open the Photos app & press **Albums,** then select **Recently Deleted** (you will find this under **Utilities).**

2. Press **Select,** click all the videos & photos you want, then click **Delete** or **Recover.**

Create a New Photo Album

Photo albums help you organize your photos. To create a new album,

1. Press **Albums** at the end of your screen.

2. Press ✛ & select **New Album.** Title your album & press **Save.**

3. Select all the photos & videos you want to move to the album & then press **Done.**

Rearrange, Rename & Delete Albums

1. Open **Photos** & click **Album** at the bottom of your screen.

2. Press **See All** & select **Edit.**

3. To rearrange, hold the album thumbnail & move it to a different location.

4. To rename, touch the album name & type in a new one.

5. To delete, press ⊖. Tap **Done** to finish.

Move Videos & Photos to an Existing Album

1. Open **Photos** & click **Library** at the bottom of your screen.

2. View **All Photos** or view by Days.

3. Press **Select** at the top & choose the content you want.

4. Tap the ⬆ icon, select **Add to Album,** & click the desired album.

Remove Content from an Album

1. Open the album & click on a photo or video, press 🗑 & choose to delete only from the album or from the device.

2. To remove more than one item, press **Select,** choose the items, & tap 🗑.

Print Photos to an AirPrint-Enabled Printer

1. To print one video, open it, press ⬆ & select **Print.**

2. To print more than one photo, click **Library,** press **All Photos,** press **Select,** & choose all the items you want to share. Press ⬆& press **Print.**

Share Photos & Videos

1. To share one video or photo, open it, press ⬆ & select a share option.

2. To share more than one content, click **Library,** press **All Photos,** press **Select,** & choose all the items you want to share. Press ⬆& select a share option.

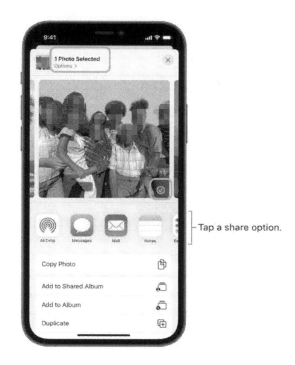

Tap a share option.

Music, Podcasts, and Video Entertainment

Your iPhone 15 is a versatile device for enjoying a wide range of audio content. Let's explore the world of music, podcasts, and audiobooks:

Music

The Apple Music app allows you to access a vast library of songs, albums, & playlists. You can also listen to your own music library if you've imported your collection into Apple Music. Here's how to enjoy music on your iPhone:

1. Open the Apple Music app.

2. Explore the "Library" to access your own music or the "Browse" section for new music.

3. Create playlists, follow artists, and discover personalized recommendations.

Podcasts

Podcasts offer a wealth of audio content on various topics. You can use the Podcasts app on your iPhone to listen to your favorite shows and discover new ones. Here's how:

1. Open the Podcasts app.

2. Browse categories, search for specific topics or titles, and subscribe to your preferred podcasts.

3. Download episodes for offline listening or stream them when connected to the internet.

Audiobooks

Audiobooks provide an enjoyable way to experience books. The Apple Books app on your iPhone allows you to purchase and listen to audiobooks. Here's how to get started:

1. Open the Apple Books app.

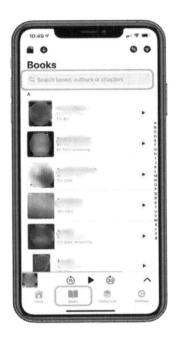  

2. Browse the audiobook store, purchase titles, and listen to them on your iPhone.

3. Adjust playback speed and use features like bookmarks to enhance your listening experience.

Watching Videos and Movies

Your iPhone 15 serves as a portable cinema, allowing you to watch videos and movies whenever and wherever you please. Here's how to enjoy visual content:

Apple TV

This app is your gateway to a world of TV shows, movies, and streaming services. You can rent or purchase movies, subscribe to streaming platforms, and watch your favorite shows. To get started:

1. Open the Apple TV app.

2. Explore the "Watch Now" section for recommendations, or browse categories for specific content.

3. Sign in your Apple ID to access your purchased or rented movies.

Streaming Apps

Your iPhone supports various streaming apps like Netflix, Amazon Prime Video, Disney+, and many others. You can download those apps from App Store and enjoy your favorite shows & movies by signing in with your account.

YouTube

This is a treasure trove of user-generated content, from entertaining vlogs to educational videos. You can download YouTube app from the App Store and start exploring.

Hobbies and Interests

Your iPhone 15 is not just a communication and entertainment device; it's a gateway to your hobbies and interests. Let's take a look at apps catering to specific interests:

- **Gardening Apps:** If you have a green thumb, gardening apps like Gardenize, iScape, or PlantSnap can help you plan and maintain your garden, identify plants, and provide useful tips on planting and caring for your greens.

- **Reading Apps:** Reading apps like Kindle, Apple Books, and Audible allow you to explore a vast library of books and audiobooks. You can purchase or borrow e-books and immerse yourself in captivating stories.

- **Travel Apps:** Travel enthusiasts can use apps like TripAdvisor, Airbnb, and Airbnb Experiences to plan their next adventure. These apps provide information on accommodations, activities, and reviews from fellow travelers.

Hobbies and Interests Apps: Whether you're into painting, cooking, birdwatching, or any other hobby, there are apps designed to support your interests. Explore the App Store to find tools, tutorials, and communities related to your passion.

Chapter 7:
Health, Wellness, and Everyday Tools

Using the Health App and Emergency Features

Health is designed as a valuable tool for seniors who appreciate staying organized with their information. This iOS application serves as a central hub, bringing together health data from various third-party apps and devices, including trackers for activities like running or steps, sleep, food diaries, mental health, reproductive health, and more.

We've compiled a list of top health accessories that seamlessly sync with the Apple Health app.

Health operates across four primary categories: activity, mindfulness, sleep, and nutrition.

By utilizing the app, you can not only enhance your data in these areas but also explore additional functionalities with the right apps. Once Health is configured properly, achieving and tracking health goals becomes more straightforward than ever for seniors.

Activity

The exercise part of Health is really handy. When you start the app and go to the exercise section, you'll find two small sections of information: your daily exercise and a summary of your whole year.

The Health app relies on your iPhone's accelerometer to track your steps & the distance you cover, as long as you have your iPhone with you for precise measurements. So, there's no need to wear a special device to get information about your steps or distance.

Stress And Mindfulness

When it comes to stress relief and mindfulness on Apple devices, the options may not be as obvious for seniors. Apple is gradually exploring this area, as seen with features like Mindful Minutes on the Apple Watch. However, to make the most of mindfulness tools, especially if you don't use an Apple Watch, you'll need to rely on third-party apps.

A recommended app for seniors is Breathe, which offers gentle reminders to take a moment and focus on your breath. You have the flexibility to set the number of reminders and the specific hours during which you'd like to receive them. For instance, if you often feel stressed during work hours, you can instruct Breathe to provide you with five reminders between 9 a.m. and 5 p.m.

In addition to the breathing reminders, Breathe also shares daily mindfulness quotes and lets you customize notifications to suit your preferences for inducing relaxation.

If Breathe doesn't resonate with you, navigate to the mindfulness section in the Health app and scroll down. There, you'll find a list of recommended apps that you can integrate into your routine. Health provides similar suggestions in its other main sections as well.

Remember to grant permission for Health to connect with any third-party app you choose. Most health, fitness, and mindfulness apps will prompt you to allow access to Health when you open them for the first time. If an app doesn't ask, you can enable the necessary permissions in your device settings.

Sleep

The simplest remedy for stress, weight concerns, lack of concentration, and not-so-great food choices – yet, it seems to be the health advice that eludes many. If you're finding it a challenge to meet your health and wellness goals, it might be worthwhile to consider how much good-quality sleep you're getting each night.

For seniors using Health, keeping tabs on your sleep is most convenient through your iPhone, Using the assistance of the Bedtime feature that is included in the Clock app, which provides built-in support. You need only set your bedtime, and your phone will send you a notification to remind you that it is time to go to sleep. Oh, and keep in mind to set an awakening time; your phone will make sure that you wake up and shine in the morning, and there is no way to trick the wake-up feature: if you reach for your phone, it will register that as your wake-up time.

While the Apple Watch doesn't come with a built-in sleep tracker for now, you can easily address that by downloading various apps. Consider the Beddit device, an Apple accessory that syncs with both your Watch and iPhone. It not only tracks your sleep duration but also monitors your heart rate, breathing, snoring, and even the conditions in your bedroom, such as temperature and humidity.

For those who prefer iPhone apps, there's a variety available to monitor your sleep, like Sleep Cycle. This app not only keeps tabs on the quality of your sleep and time spent in different sleep stages but also aims to wake you up during the lightest sleep stage to help you start your day without that groggy feeling.

Food And Nutrition

Although it may not be the most enjoyable task, keeping track of our food intake is beneficial. However, for seniors, especially, manually monitoring every detail, such as calcium or iron content, can be tedious and time-consuming.

A more convenient option is to utilize the nutrition feature in Health, where you can input your food intake. Nevertheless, this approach requires entering every detail, even the milligram amounts of nutrients like sodium.

For seniors, third-party apps like MyFitnessPal or Lifesum can make the process easier. These apps synchronize with Health, and their extensive food databases include nutrient breakdowns for most meals and snacks. By using such apps, seniors can access a comprehensive overview of their macronutrient and micronutrient intake for the day, month, and year, either through integration with Health or manual data entry.

Import Health Records

For seniors seeking convenient access to their medical records, the Health app could be a useful tool, depending on your healthcare provider. Apple introduced a feature in 2018, starting with iOS 11.3, which enables users to bring in their health data from their doctor or clinic.

With almost 100 clinic and hospital locations supporting this functionality, you can explore and view information and records such as immunizations, medications, blood pressure, allergies, hospital visits, test results, and more, if your healthcare provider is among those offering this service.

Set up a Medical ID

Remember those emergency contact cards people used to carry? Well, imagine having a digital version on your phone that could be a lifesaver in case of a medical or other emergency. That's what your Medical ID on Apple Health is all about.

In the event that you have your Medical ID configured in Health, it will be possible for paramedics, first responders, and other individuals to easily access vital information directly from your home screen. Without even having to unlock your phone, they can accomplish this by tapping "Emergency" and then "Medical ID" on your cellular device. As a precaution to protect your privacy, this function is disabled by default.

Your Medical ID can share important details about you. You can input your basic information like age, gender, height, and weight. Additionally, you can include details about your medical conditions, medications, and allergies. Don't forget to list your emergency contacts and their phone numbers on your Medical ID.

Here's how to set up your Medical ID:

1. First, launch the Health app and select the "Medical ID" item from the menu.

2. When you are on the edit screen, select your contact card from the list of contacts on your iPhone. This will allow Medical ID to know who you are.

3. Enter any information you desire, especially your blood type, allergies, emergency contacts, and organ donor status, among other pertinent details.

4. You should enable "Show When Locked" by toggling the switch to the green position. This will allow other people to view your Medical ID card right from the lock screen of your iPhone.

Everyone with an iPhone should complete their Medical ID—it could make a significant difference in an emergency.

Satellite-Based Emergency SOS on iPhone 15

For iPhone 15 users, the Emergency SOS feature now extends to satellite connectivity, allowing you to send texts to emergency services in situations where cellular and Wi-Fi coverage is unavailable.

Note: Satellite-based Emergency SOS may not be accessible in all countries or regions. Refer to the Apple Support article on Emergency SOS via satellite availability for details.

Before venturing into areas without coverage:

If you anticipate being in an area without cellular or Wi-Fi, take proactive steps:

1. Set up your Medical ID and include emergency contacts.

2. Familiarize yourself with the Emergency SOS feature by going to Settings > Emergency SOS and selecting "Try Demo."

To establish your Medical ID and add emergency contacts, refer to the instructions for setting up Medical ID.

Note: The Emergency SOS demo does not initiate a call to emergency services.

Initiate Emergency SOS via satellite on your iPhone:

In situations where you require emergency assistance without cellular or Wi-Fi access, you can utilize Emergency SOS via satellite.

1. Attempt to call 911 or emergency services. Even if your regular cellular network is unavailable, your iPhone will attempt to route the call through alternate networks.

2. If the call fails, tap "Emergency Text via Satellite" to send a text to emergency services. Alternatively, open the Messages app, text 911 or SOS, and then tap "Emergency Services."

3. Tap "Report Emergency" and follow the onscreen instructions.

Important: Ensure a clear line of sight to the sky when attempting to connect to a satellite. Hold your phone naturally, without raising your arm. In obstructed environments, such as heavy foliage, successful satellite connection may be impeded.

Once connected, your iPhone initiates a text conversation, sharing vital information such as your Medical ID, emergency contacts, responses to the emergency questionnaire, location (including elevation), and battery level. Additionally, you have the option to share this information with your designated emergency contacts.

Fitness Tracking and Wellness Tips

With the Fitness app, you can effortlessly track your daily activity, set personalized move goals, monitor your progress, and observe movement trends over time, even if you do not own an Apple Watch.

Tracking Your Progress:

1. Open the Fitness app at any time to assess your performance.

2. View essential metrics such as your Move ring, total steps, completed workouts, trends, and more.

3. When your iPhone accompanies you, motion sensors record steps, distance, and flights climbed, estimating active calories burned. Workouts completed in compatible third-party apps also contribute to your Move ring progress.

4. An overlapping ring indicates that you have surpassed your daily goal. Tap the Activity area to delve into the details of your achievements for the day.

Adjusting Move Goal or Personal Health Details

1. Open the Fitness app on your iPhone.

2. Tap your profile picture or initials located at the top right.

3. Take the following actions: • To modify your move goal, tap "Change Goals," adjust the goal using the provided controls, and then tap "Change Move Goal."

• To update health details, tap "Health Details," make necessary changes by tapping a field, and then tap "Done." • Alternatively, navigate to the Activity area, scroll down, and tap "Change Goals."

Weekly Notifications and Goal Adjustments: Every Monday, receive a notification summarizing your achievements from the previous week, along with suggested goals for the upcoming week based on your performance. Take this opportunity to fine-tune your objectives to better align with your fitness journey.

Calendar, Reminders, Notes, and Voice Memos

Calendar App

Unlock the potential of the iOS Calendar app by discovering its concealed tools and features beneath the surface. Over the years, Apple's calendar app has evolved significantly from its initial launch, offering a more refined and feature-rich experience.

To maximize your usage of the app, follow these steps to explore its functionalities and uncover some hidden gems.

Getting Started and Unveiling Hidden Features

Apple's Calendar app is designed to be user-friendly, providing a straightforward entry point with the option for deeper exploration. Here's a guide on how to initiate your journey and unearth features you might not be aware of.

Creating and personalizing your calendar can be done in the following manner.

1. Open the Calendar app and tap on "Calendar" at the bottom center of the screen.

2. Select "Add Calendar" located at the bottom left of the screen.

3. Choose between adding a regular calendar (for personal customization), a subscription calendar (via link), or a holiday calendar (linked to a specific region's holidays).

4. Opt for "Add Calendar" to initiate customization.

5. Provide your calendar with a name that suits your preference.

6. Choose the account to which you want the calendar connected (Outlook, Gmail, or iCloud).

7. Select a color for your calendar to help it stand out among others.

Although Apple sets a default calendar for you during the initial device setup, you have the option to customize your experience by choosing a different default calendar. This selected calendar, while changeable later, becomes the default choice when creating a new event within the app.

Here's how to set your default calendar:

1. Navigate to Settings and scroll down until you find Calendar.

2. Tap on Calendar and then select "Default Calendar."

3. Choose the calendar that you want to set as your default.

Creating calendars tailored to specific activities or groups is a practical approach to maintaining a well-organized schedule for both personal and group events. The ability to assign different colors to each calendar, with the option to choose any color you prefer, adds a visual element that aids in quickly identifying events associated with particular activities or groups.

Calendars that you create will be located within the account you have selected to align with the respective calendar.

How to share a calendar

Creating a calendar doesn't have to be a solo endeavor; you can easily involve others by sending invitations. This enables multiple individuals to view and contribute to the shared calendar. Here's a step-by-step guide on how to create collaborative calendars with others:

1. Open the Calendar app and navigate to "Calendars" at the bottom.

2. Secondly, you will need to create a new calendar within your iCloud account because other accounts will not permit you to share it using the Calendar app.

3. Once the calendar is created, locate it in your list of calendars under iCloud and tap on it.

4. Select "Ad Person."

5. Enter the person's name or email address to send them an invitation to collaborate on the calendar. You can specify whether they can view & edit the calendar or only view it.

6. Once they accept the invitation, they gain the permissions you granted.

7. If you wish to stop sharing calendar with specific individuals, tap on their name and choose "Stop Sharing."

When sharing the calendar, you have the option to choose a color, making it easier to distinguish from events in your other calendars.

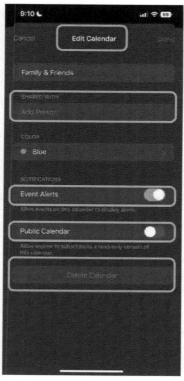
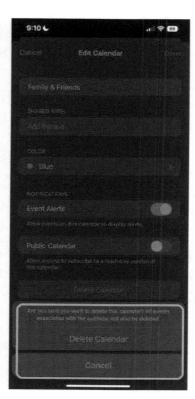

Enable the "Show Changes" option to receive notifications when individuals sharing the calendar add, modify, or remove events. You can also set the calendar to Public, allowing anyone with the shareable link to view it without editing permissions.

If you prefer not to receive event alerts, simply disable the "Event Alerts" toggle in the calendar's settings. Sharing calendars with family and friends offers an enjoyable way to stay informed about their plans, facilitating coordination for trips, dinners, or quality time together.

Gone are the days of asking "are you free?" Now, you can effortlessly check the shared calendar to plan activities and spend meaningful time with your loved ones. It's a fantastic way to prioritize time with those who matter most to you.

Reminder App
reminder.

Additionally, you can conveniently add reminders to your crucial to-do lists directly from the

Create a Reminder

1. Launch the Reminders app.

2. Select + New Reminder and input your reminder.

Additionally, you can conveniently add reminders to your crucial to-do lists directly from the Reminders widget on your Home Screen.

Establish a Deadline

Select the Date and Time button to specify a due date for your reminder. Options include Today, Tomorrow, This Weekend, or you can tap Date & Time to set a custom day and time.

If you set a due date without assigning a specific time, the notification defaults to 9:00 AM. To adjust the default time for all-day reminders, navigate to the Settings app, then tap Reminders. Choose a different time by tapping the time below All-Day Reminders.

Include a Location

Tap the Location button to associate a notification with your current whereabouts. Choose from provided options or tap Custom to input your own location details.

Specify whether you want to be notified upon arrival or departure, and set the reminder area's perimeter.

For location-based reminders, ensure Location Services is enabled. Open the Settings app, then access Privacy & Security > Location Services, and turn on Location Services.

Attach a Tag

Select the Tag button to attach a keyword-based tag to your reminder. Tags facilitate quick and automatic organization of reminders.

Highlight a Reminder

Tap the Flag button to designate a reminder as especially significant, prompting it to be featured in the Flagged smart list on the main screen of the Reminders app.

Attach a File

Tap the Photos button to include an attachment with your reminder. Options include taking a new photo, choosing an image from your photo library, or scanning a document.

Modify a Reminder

You may add additional data and adjustments to your reminder by tapping the Edit data button. Some examples of these are notes, a URL, and priority. Furthermore, you have the ability to modify the notification settings of the reminder and alter the list to which it is assigned.

Get a Reminder While Messaging Someone

1. Select a reminder and then click on the Edit Details button.

2. Activate the When Messaging option.

3. Choose a person by tapping on Choose Person, and select a name from your contacts.

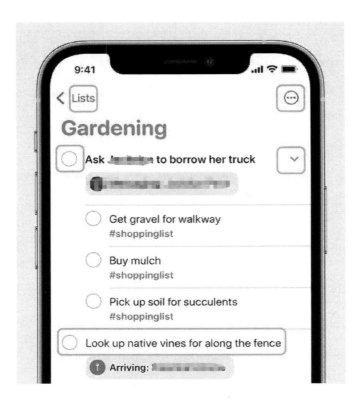

Upon your next conversation with this individual in Messages, a Reminders notification will be displayed.

Create Subtasks

Each reminder you generate has the capability to include subtasks. For instance, a reminder to prepare for a trip can encompass a checklist of essential items to remember. You can create subtasks using various methods:

1. Long-press a reminder, then drag and drop it onto another reminder. The dragged reminder becomes a subtask of the destination reminder.

2. Swipe right on a reminder, then select "Indent." This action transforms the reminder into a subtask of the one immediately above it. To reverse this, swipe right again on the subtask and choose "Outdent."

3. Tap a reminder, click the "Edit Details" button , select "Subtasks," then choose "Add Reminder" and input your subtask. Repeat this process for as many subtasks as needed.

4. If subtasks cannot be generated, ensure you are utilizing iCloud Reminders.

Complete a Reminder

To mark a reminder as accomplished, tap the empty circle beside it. To view completed reminders, click the "More" button, then select "Show Completed."

If you want to get rid of a reminder without labeling it as finished, swipe left on the reminder, and then hit the "Delete" button. In the event that you come across a notification for a reminder on your Lock Screen, swipe left over the reminder, press "View," and then select "Mark as Completed."

Create a Reminder Using Siri

Utilize Siri to set up reminders on your iOS device or Apple Watch.* Below are a few illustrative examples:

- "Schedule a daily reminder at 7:30 a.m. to feed the dog."
- "Set a reminder for when I arrive home to check the mail."
- "Create a reminder to stop by the grocery store when I leave this location."

Enhance Siri's ability to assist you with location-based reminders by adding your home and work addresses to your Contacts card. Navigate to the Contacts app, select My Card, tap Edit, add your work or home address, and then tap Done.

Siri utilizes Location Services for reminders requiring your location. Siri's availability, features, and commands may vary based on language, country, and region.

Set a Reminder From a Different App

If you need to remind yourself to return to another app, such as revisiting a website or map location, incorporate a link in your reminder pointing to where you left off. Open the desired app, locate the Share button, and then select the Reminders icon.

Notes App

The Notes app is a robust and intricate application with a plethora of features. Here are some guidelines on utilizing both the fundamental and advanced functionalities, including encrypting notes, drawing within notes, syncing notes to iCloud, and more.

Creating a New Note in the iPhone Notes App

To create a basic note in the Notes app, follow these steps:

1. Open the Notes app by tapping its icon.

2. Tap "Add Note," represented by a pencil and a piece of paper icon in the lower-right corner.

3. Utilize the on-screen keyboard to input your note.

4. After typing, tap "Done."

5. Navigate to the top of the screen then tap "Notes" to return to Notes home screen.

By default, the note receives a filename that combines the date (or time) and the initial few words of the note, positioning it at the top of the notes list.

Formatting Text in iPhone Notes

Enhance the visual appeal & organization of your notes by incorporating text formatting. Here's a step-by-step guide:

1. Open the desired note by tapping on it.

2. When you tap on a line of text within the note, the keyboard and a menu for formatting will appear on the screen. Grids, text formatting, checklists, and colors are all visual representations that can be found on this menu. Tapping

the plus sign located in the upper-right corner of the keyboard will bring up the formatting menu if it is not already accessible.

3. Tap "Aa" to access the text-formatting options.

4. Choose the text you want to format, and then make adjustments to the handles to specify the portion of the text. Make use of the various options that are accessible when formatting text, including bold, italic, underlined, and strike-through, as well as alignment, bullet points, and other possibilities.

5. Tap "Done" when you have completed the text formatting.

Creating a Checklist in an iPhone Note

Utilize the Notes app to effortlessly generate checklists with the following steps:

1. Open an existing note or initiate a new one. Tap anywhere within the note to bring up the keyboard.

2. Above the keyboard, tap the "+" icon to reveal the formatting tools.

3. To highlight the full item on the list, press and hold the item you want to highlight, and then move the handles. The next step is to tap the checkmark icon, which will cause a circle to appear in front of the object that has been selected.

4. Press "Return" on the keyboard to add another checklist item. If necessary, tap the checklist icon and continue this process until your entire list is created.

5. As you complete each item on the checklist, tap within the circle in front of it to mark it as done.

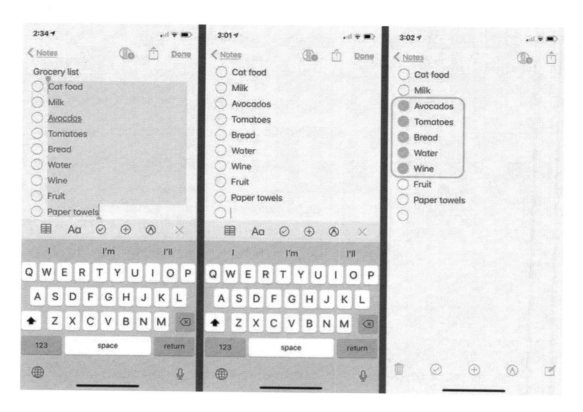

Drawing in Your Notes on iPhone

For those who prefer visual representation, you can easily sketch in your notes on iPhone. Follow these steps:

1. In an open note, tap pen icon above the keyboard. For iOS 17, it's the pen icon.

2. Explore the drawing options, which may vary depending on your iOS version:

   o **Tool:** Choose from a pencil, marker, pen, or eraser. Tap a tool to select or deselect it.

   o **Color:** Change the line color by tapping the black dot on the right.

   o **Undo and Redo:** Correct mistakes or redo actions by tapping the curved arrows next to Done button.

   o **Create a Second Page:** Tap square icon with a plus sign to add a new page. Navigate between pages by swiping with two fingers.

   o **Tables:** Insert a table by tapping the grid icon. Edit rows or columns by selecting "More (...)". Add content to a table cell by tapping it.

Attaching Photos and Videos to Notes on iPhone

Enhance your notes by including more than just text. Follow these steps to quickly attach photos and videos:

1. Open the note where you want to add the attachment.

2. Tap within the body of the note to reveal the options above the keyboard.

3. In iOS 17, tap the "+" icon in the toolbar above the keyboard.

4. Choose the "Take Photo or Video" to capture a new item, or select "Photo Library" to pick an existing file.

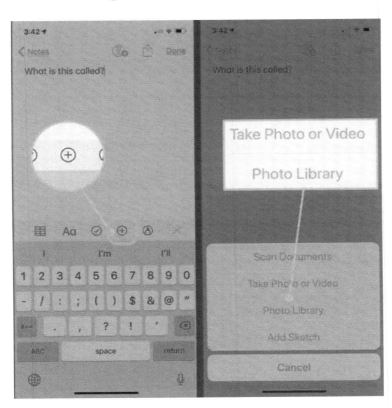

5. When you select "Take Photo or Video," the camera app will launch on your device. "Use Photo" or "Use Video" should be selected after the photo or video has been captured. You are now able to view or play the photo (or video) that has been contributed to the remark.

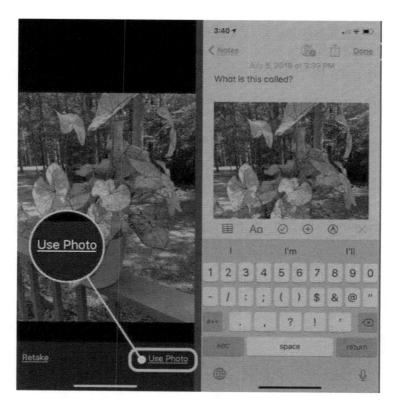

6. If you choose "Photo Library," navigate through the Photos app, select the desired photo or video, and tap "Choose" to attach it to the note.

Scanning Documents in iPhone Notes

Utilize the built-in document scanning feature in the Notes app for iOS 17 to effortlessly save receipts or other documents. Follow these steps:

1. In an open note, access the formatting toolbar above the keyboard by tapping the + icon.

2. Select "Scan Documents."

3. In camera view, position the document on-screen to be surrounded by a yellow outline.

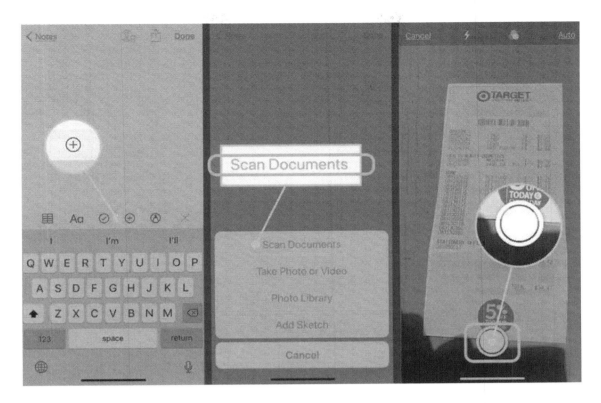

7. Tap the large circular button to reveal a cropping grid marked by a white outline. Adjust circles at the corners of the grid to align the white line with the document's edge.

8. Choose either "Keep Scan" or "Retake." If you opt for "Keep Scan" and it's the only scan needed, tap "Save."

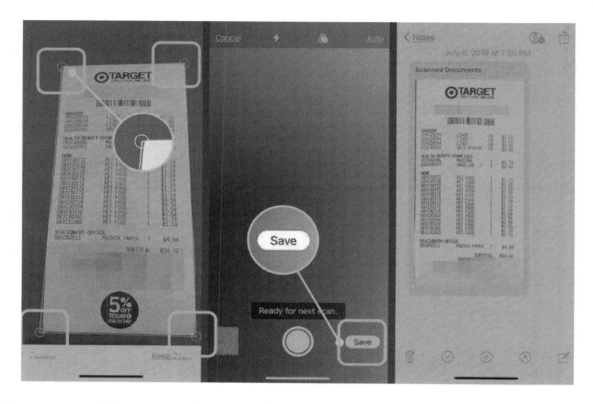

9. The scanned document is now added to your note.

Sharing Notes on iPhone

While Notes are a great personal tool, sharing them with others is easy. To share a note on your iPhone:

1. Open the note you wish to share.

2. Tap the Share icon, typically represented by a square with an arrow pointing out. This action will display a window with various sharing options, including:

   o **AirDrop:** You can use Bluetooth and Wi-Fi to send the note wirelessly to a different iPhone, iPad, or Mac via wireless transmission. Master the art of using AirDrop on your iPhone.

   o **Message:** Send a text message to yourself that contains the contents of the note. The encrypted iMessage technology is utilized whenever it is possible to send a message to a different Apple device.

- **Mail:** You can convert the note into an email by using the Mail app on your iPhone, which will open the email in its default format.

- **Save Image:** If you have an image that is attached to a note, you can use this option to save the image to the Photos app on your device. This choice will just save the image, not the full note.

- **Print:** If you are in close proximity to a printer that is compatible with AirPrint, you can wirelessly transfer the note to the printer in order to obtain a quick hard copy.

- **Assign to Contact:** This option, which is applicable to photos that are attached to notes, gives you the ability to assign an image that is contained within a note to a person in your Contacts app so that they have that image as their default photo.

Choose sharing option that best suits your needs, and effortlessly distribute your notes to others or store them in different formats.

Voice Memo App

Your iPhone 15 comes equipped with a convenient built-in application for capturing impromptu audio moments at any time. The Voice Memos app on your iPhone serves as an excellent choice for documenting interviews, quick musical snippets, spontaneous thoughts, and more. With no predetermined time constraints on your recordings, just ensure your device has ample storage capacity.

How To Record a Voice Memo on Your iPhone

1. Launch the Voice Memos app and press the red Record button.

2. As the recording progresses, a dynamic waveform will be visible.

3. Press red Stop button to conclude the recording.

4. Your recorded audio will be stored in the list of All Recordings.

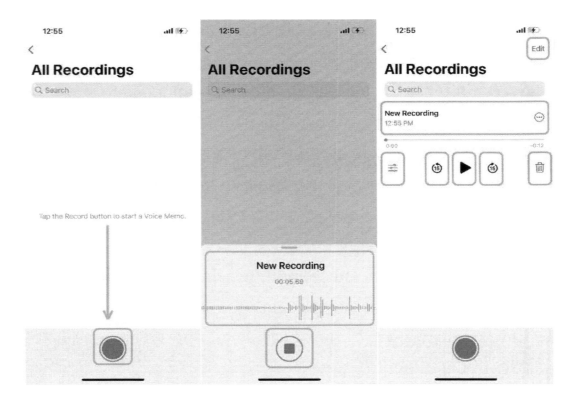

How to Playback a Recorded Voice Memo in the Voice Memos App

Once you've captured a voice memo on your iPhone, it's time to listen to the recording. Here's a step-by-step guide:

1. Open the Voice Memos app to view your list of recordings.

2. Locate and tap on the saved recording in the All-Recordings list.

3. Press the Play button to start playback.

4. To navigate to a specific point, use the slider. Alternatively, utilize the Fast-Forward or Rewind buttons to skip ahead or go back by 15 seconds.

For additional playback options, tap the Options button (depicted as three sliders). Here, you'll find other features you can use during playback:

o Playback Speed: Adjust the speed by dragging towards the turtle for slower playback or towards the rabbit for faster playback.

o Skip Silence: This feature automatically skips over periods of silence in your recording.

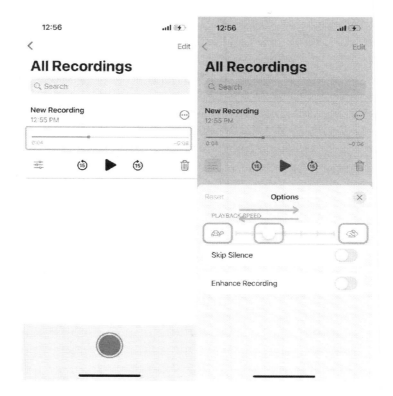

How to Delete and Restore Voice Memos

To remove a voice memo you no longer require, follow these steps:

1. Simply tap Trash icon to delete the selected voice memo.

If you accidentally delete a recording and wish to recover it, here's how:

1. Navigate to the All-Recordings page.

2. Tap the Back arrow to access the Recently Deleted section.

3. Choose the recording you want to restore and tap Recover.

4. Confirm by tapping Recover Recording.

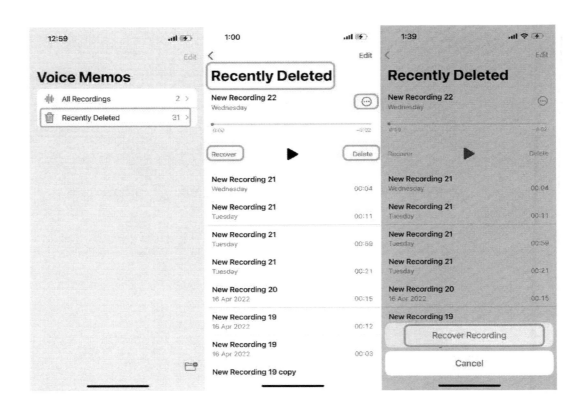

Chapter 8:
Navigating and Exploring

Using Maps for Navigation

Utilize Apple Maps for effective outing planning and secure navigation. Whether you're seeking directions to reunite with your grandchildren or meeting friends for lunch at an unfamiliar restaurant, this application has your back. Explore the following step-by-step guide to maximize the utility of this app. Discover how to locate a destination, navigate to it, share your location, employ Siri for guidance, and customize Apple Maps to align with your preferences.

Open Apple Maps

Opening the app can be done in a couple of ways:

- Easily access it by tapping the app icon located anywhere on your homescreen.
- Swipe right from your homescreen to access your today view, then tap "Apple Maps."

- If you click on an address from a website, text message, or email, Apple Maps should automatically open to that specific location.

Add Important Addresses

Upon opening the app, you'll encounter a list of "Favorites," offering a convenient way to save time on frequent addresses. This feature allows you to store your home address and other frequently used locations for quick access, eliminating the need to input the complete address every time you require directions. Here's a step-by-step guide on how to add addresses to your favorites:

1. Tap on either "Home," "Work," or "Add."

2. The app will prompt you to access your contact card on your phone.

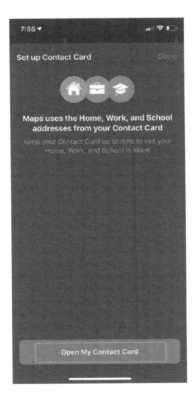

3. Input the address you wish to add to your favorites then click "Done" in the top right corner once you've finished.

Pin and Share Your Location

You have the option to mark your current location on the map or share it with others, which can be useful for remembering where you parked or providing your location to someone picking you up. Follow these steps:

1. Tap the "i" icon.

2. Next, tap "Mark my Location." This action will place a red pin on the map, indicating the selected location.

3. Press the "Share" icon to send your location to someone else through a message.

4. If you no longer need the marked location, tap the red pin and choose "Remove" to clear it from the map.

View Nearby Locations

Apple Maps proves highly valuable for discovering nearby amenities. Whether you're in search of a restaurant, store, gas station, or repair shop, the Maps app provides comprehensive information for your needs. Here's a simple guide:

1. Tap the search bar and either:

   o Choose a category from the "Find Nearby" options.

o Type or dictate a specific category such as "urgent care."

2. Select a business or location to view detailed information, including:

- Address
- Directions
- Contact information, with a click-to-call option
- Hours of operation
- Yelp reviews and menus
- Photos & a 360-degree view of the exterior

Get Directions to a Location

After deciding on your destination, Apple Maps facilitates navigation from either your current location or a specified one. Follow these steps:

1. Tap "Directions."

2. Select your preferred mode of transportation by touching the icon that corresponds to it, whether it be driving, walking, taking public transportation, riding a bicycle, or using a ride-sharing service.

3. Under the "Avoid" section, tap "Tolls" or "Highways" if desired. The grey slider button turning green indicates a successful selection. Apple Maps will then adjust the route based on your preferences, allowing you to avoid tolls or highways.

4. Apple Maps often provides multiple routes to your destination. To select a route:

- Toggle between different routes on the map by tapping the various blue lines.

o Alternatively, choose a route from options below the map by tapping on a route from list. This provides turn-by-turn directions.

5. Once you've settled on the route of your choice, tap "Go" to commence navigation.

Add a New Stop to Your Route

If you need to make a stop during your journey, you can easily add one while navigating. This is particularly useful for long road trips when you need to refuel or grab a meal along the way. Here's how:

1. Choose the sort of location you are looking for by tapping the "Route" card located at the bottom of the screen. There are a variety of options available, including restaurants, petrol stations, and coffee shops.

2. Options near your route will be presented both on the map and in a list format.

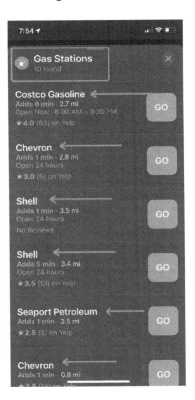

3. Tap "Go" next to one of the options to initiate navigation to that location.

4. Once you have completed your stop, or if you have changed your mind and don't desire to proceed with the extra stop, you can keep on your original route by tapping the "Resume Route" button with the blue color at the top of the screen.

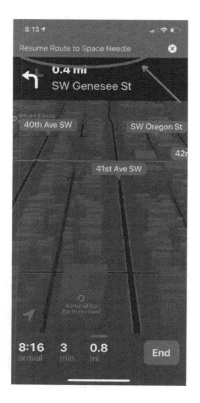

End Navigation

1. To conclude your navigation, tap the red "End" icon.

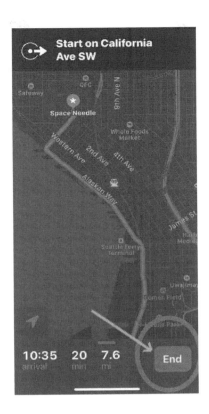

2. Then, confirm your decision by tapping "End Route."

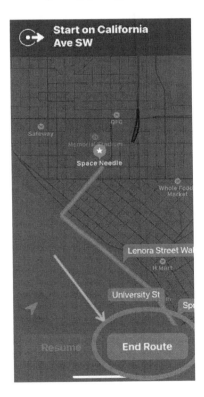

163

Use Siri to Get Directions

When it comes to receiving directions on Maps, using Siri is particularly helpful because it provides a more rapid choice. If you find it difficult to type or read on your smartphone, you can use Siri instead. You have the ability to offer orders such as "Give me walking directions home" or "Give me directions to Ann's house." Proceed with the following instructions if Siri has not yet been activated:

1. Open your "Settings" app and tap "Siri & Search."

2. Ensure that the toggle icons under the "Ask Siri" header are turned on. They will turn from gray to green when enabled.

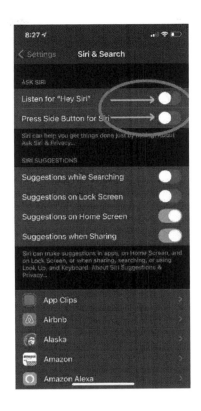

Browsing the Internet Safely

Surf the Web on Safari

Pinch open or closed to zoom.

Enter a web address or search term, or quickly access your Favorites.

View open tabs and Tab Groups, or open a new tab.

Open the Share menu for more options.

165

1. Open the Safari app ⬤ from the app library or home screen.

2. Enter web address in the address field or enter a search phrase to get options.

3. Double press the top edge of your screen to return to the top of the app screen from any part of the page.

4. Pull down from the topmost edge of the page to refresh the page.

5. Rotate your iPhone 15 to landscape to view more content on the page.

6. Press ⬆️ at the end of a webpage to share the web link.

7. Press & hold a link in Safari for a preview of the web page without launching the page.

8. Click the preview or select **Open** to go to the web page.

9. To remain on the current page & exit the preview, touch anywhere outside the preview space.

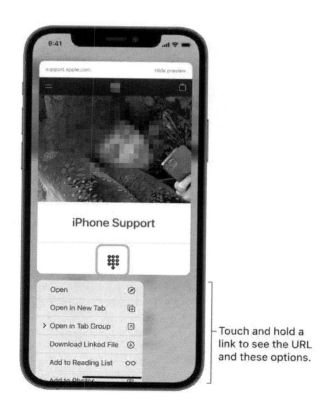

Touch and hold a link to see the URL and these options.

Add Safari to Your Home Screen

If you can't find the Safari app on your home screen but want it there, use the steps below to add it back:

1. Go to the App Library & search for 'Safari' in the search field or swipe to the app.

2. Then touch & hold the app icon 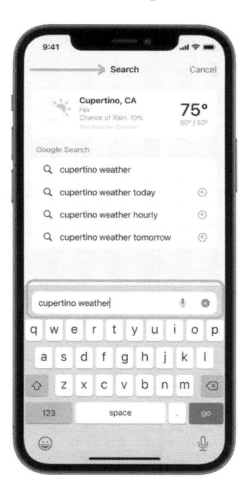 & press **Add to Home Screen.**

Search the Web

In Safari, you can use the search field to go directly to a website by inputting the website URL or entering a search term to find the information across multiple websites.

1. Open the Safari app & click the search space.

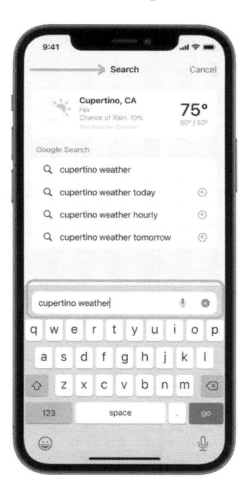

2. Type the URL in the search space or enter a search phrase.

3. If searching using a phrase, click a suggestion to go to it or click **Go** on your keyboard to search specifically for the term you entered.

Select Default Search Engine

1. In Settings app on your iPhone ◉, click **Safari.**

2. Click **Search Engine** & make your choice.

Translate a Webpage

Use Safari to get the translated version of a page.

1. Click ᴬA on the webpage, then click 🔤.

2. Note that not all languages are available for this service.

Change Screen Layout in Safari

You can change the screen layout to another type. Your selection will determine the location of the search bar – the Tab Bar layout keeps the search bar at the bottom of your screen, while the Single Tap layout keeps the bar at the top. Choose a layout with the steps below:

1. Scroll to the left side of the search field & press ᴬA.

2. Then select an option: '**Show Bottom Tab Bar**' or '**Show Top Address Bar.**'

3. In Settings app on your iPhone ◉, click **Safari.**

4. Swipe to **Tabs** & select an option: '**Single Tab**' or '**Tab Bar.**'

Customize Your Start Page

Customize the Safari start page to have new background images & other options.

1. Open a new tab, press ⧉, & then press +.

2. Swipe to the end of the app screen & press **Edit.**

3. Now you can customize/ turn on options for your Safari start page:

   o Favorites – find a shortcut to websites you marked as favorites on the start page.

   o Siri Suggestions – turn this on so that Siri can suggest webpages as you search.

   o Shared with You – to view links that people shared with you in Mail, Messages, & other apps.

   o Frequently Visited – see the list of your frequently visited websites here.

   o Privacy Report – for a report of the number of websites & trackers that Safari blocked from tracking your web activity.

   o Reading List – see a list of pages in your Reading List.

   o iCloud Tabs – to see other open tabs from all your other Apple devices that are linked to the same Apple ID as your iPhone 15.

o Note that changes to the start page settings will apply to all your linked Apple devices using the same Apple ID.

Change Text Size

Increase or decrease the size of text on a website.

1. Scroll to the left side of the search field & press ᴬA.

2. Use the small A to reduce the text size & the big A to increase it.

Open a Link in a New Tab

When you come across links on a webpage, you can choose to open them on a new tab.

1. Press & hold the new link, then select **Open in New Tab.**

When you open a link in a new tab, the iPhone will automatically take you to the new screen. However, you can change the setting to remain on the current tab:

1. In Settings app on your iPhone 🔘 , click **Safari.**

2. Click **Open Links** & then click **In Background.**

Search Within Websites

You can search for a term within a website. For example, you can enter "crypto amazon" to go straight to all crypto-related results on Amazon. Use the steps below to turn this setting on:

1. In Settings app on your iPhone 🔘 , click **Safari.**

2. Then switch on **Quick Website Search.**

Search the Page

To find a specific phrase or words on a webpage,

1. Click ⬆& select **Find on Page.**

2. Type the phrase or words in the search box & press ⌄to jump to the different mentions of that word.

Browse Open Tabs

See all open tabs on one page and navigate through them.

1. Click ⧉in the Safari app & click ⊗in the top right side of the preview to close a tab.

2. To open a tab, click it or click **Done** to return to the single tab.

Reopen Recently Closed Tabs

1. Click ⧉in the Safari app, press +& click any of the recently closed tabs.

See Your Favorite Websites in Search or New Tabs

This setting will allow you to see your favorite websites when you click the search field or open a new tab. To turn on,

1. In Settings app on your iPhone ⚙, click **Safari.**

2. Click **Favorites** & select the folder that should show in the categories above.

View All Open Tabs Across your Other Devices

All devices must be signed in to iCloud using the same Apple ID.

1. In Settings app on your iPhone ⚙, click your name.

2. Click **iCloud** & switch on **Safari.**

3. Click ⧉in the Safari app, press +, & then swipe to see all the open tabs.

4. To delete a tab from the list, press & hold that link & then select **Choose.** The link will be removed from your iPhone 15 but not from the original device.

Organize Your Tabs

You can use a Tab group to organize your tabs & make it easy to return to them later.

1. Click ⧉ in the Safari app to see your open tabs.

2. Press & hold one tab & select **Move to Tab Group.**

3. Click **New Tab Group** & title the group.

4. Click ⌄ in the lower section of your screen to move between Tab Groups.

Move a Tab to Another Group

1. Click ⧉ in the Safari app to see your open tabs.

2. Press & hold one tab to move it. When you see a menu option, click **Move to Tab Group.**

3. Select an existing group or create a new one.

Close All Open Tabs

1. Press & hold the ⬜ icon on a page, then click **Close All Tabs.**

Add Pages to Bookmark

Bookmarks are perfect for pages you want to save and read later/

1. Open the webpage, click ⬆ & select **Add Bookmark.**

View & Organize Your Bookmarks

1. Click 📖 in Safari to view your bookmarks.

2. To organize, click **Edit** & click an option on your screen:

   o Create a new folder

   o Rename bookmarks

   o Delete bookmarks

   o Reorder bookmarks

Create Your Favorites Lists

1. Open the webpage, click ⬆ & select **Add to Favorites.**

Edit Your Favorites Lists

1. Click 📖 in Safari & click **Favorites.**

2. Then click **Edit** to rename, delete, or rearrange your favorites.

Add Pages to/ View your Reading List

Just like bookmarks, add pages you want to read later to your reading list. To add the current webpage,

1. Click 📖 in Safari & select Add to Reading List.

2. To view the list, press 📖 & then press 👓.

3. Swipe a list to the left to delete it from the reading list.

Show Readers

Reader blocks all ads and navigation menus on a webpage

Tap to view the
page in Reader.

1. Press ᴬA & click **Show Reader.**

2. Press ᴬA & click **Hide Reader** to return to the full page.

Show Reader isn't available on a website if the option is dimmed.

Save a Webpage as a PDF

Before you save a webpage, you can write & draw notes, highlight your favorite parts, & make other edits.

1. Press ⬆ on the webpage to begin saving.

2. To write & make a selection on the webpage, press **Markup** Ⓐ, select your tool & make your changes.

3. Press **Done** & continue with the onscreen instructions.

View Shared Links on Your Start Page

When friends share links with you in Messages, you can see them on your start page. You must have saved the friend as a contact on your iPhone 15. Then turn on Safari for messages with the steps below:

1. In Settings app on your iPhone ◉ , click **Messages.**

2. Then switch on **Shared with You.**

Once this is turned on, continue with the steps below:

1. Click ⬒ in the Safari app, press ＋ to launch a new tab.

2. Click **Edit** down the page & switch on **Shared with You.**

3. Once you turn on this option, you will find your shared links on this screen. To reorder your start page, press & drag the ☰ icon to a new location.

4. Click a link to open it.

Remove shared links from Shared with You

1. Find the link you want to remove in the Shared with You screen, press & hold the preview image of that link.

2. Then click **Remove Link.**

Automatically Use Reader for a Website

Customize a website to always use Reader (block ads & distraction menus).

1. Press ᴬA on a supported website & click **Website Settings.**

2. Then switch on **Use Reader Automatically**

You can also turn this setting for all supported websites.

1. In Settings app on your iPhone ◉ , click **Safari.**

2. Click **Reader** & switch on the menu.

Block Pop-Ups

1. In Settings app on your iPhone ⚙, click **Safari.**

2. Then switch on **Block Pop-ups.**

View Privacy Report

This gives a report of the number of websites & trackers that Safari blocked from tracking your web activity. To get the report,

1. Press ᴬA & select 🛡**Privacy Report**.

Use Private Browsing Mode

Private browsing mode allows you to browse without making history. That is, your activities aren't tracked & won't appear on your history.

1. Open Safari & click ⊡.

2. Click ⌄ in the bottom of your screen (in the center of the Tab bar), then select **Private.**

To exit private browsing mode,

1. Click ⊡ & press ⌄ to see the different Tab Group, click on a group outside the Private Group to exit this mode.

Clear Cache in Safari

By clearing the cache, you are deleting website history & recent searches from your iPhone 15

1. In Settings app on your iPhone ⚙, click **Safari.**

2. **Then select** 'Clear History & Website Data.'

Exploring Additional Apps and Features

The App Store

The App Store is your one-stop destination for discovering, downloading, and updating apps on your iPhone 15. It's a virtual marketplace filled with a vast selection of apps that cater to an array of interests and needs. Whether you're seeking productivity tools, entertainment, or utilities, the App Store has you covered. Here's an overview of how to navigate the App Store:

- **Accessing App Store:** To access the App Store, just tap the "App Store" icon on your home screen. The icon is easily identifiable with a blue background and a white letter "A."

- **Home Page:** The App Store's home page showcases featured apps, curated collections, and trending categories. It's an excellent place to discover new and popular apps.

- **Search:** Utilize search bar located at the bottom of your screen to locate specific apps. You can search by app name, category, or relevant keywords.

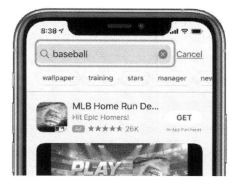

- **Categories:** Tap "Categories" to explore apps organized into various categories such as "Games," "Health & Fitness," "Education," and many more.

- **Today:** The "Today" tab provides app recommendations, reviews, and articles highlighting noteworthy apps and games.

- **Updates:** Under the "Updates" tab, you can view then install available updates for your installed apps.

- **Account:** Your Apple ID profile icon is located in the upper right corner. Here, you can access your account settings, purchased apps, and more.

- **App Details:** When you select an app, you'll see its details page, featuring an app description, screenshots, user reviews, and ratings. You can also tap the "Get" button to download free apps or the price button for paid apps.

- **Install and Updates:** To install an app, tap the "Get" or price button. If it's a paid app, you'll need to confirm the purchase with your Apple ID password or Face ID/Touch ID. To update apps, navigate to the "Updates" tab, and tap "Update" next to the app's name.

- **Wish List:** You can add apps to your Wish List for future consideration. To do so, tap the Share icon on an app's details page and select "Add to Wish List."

- **Redeem Gift Cards and Promo Codes:** If you have App Store gift cards or promo codes, you can redeem them by scrolling to the bottom of the "Today" tab and selecting "Redeem Gift Card or Code."

- **In-App Purchases and Subscriptions:** Be aware that some apps offer in-app purchases and subscriptions. You can manage these under "Settings" > "iTunes & App Store" > "Subscriptions."

Downloading and Organizing Apps
Downloading Apps:

3. **Access the App Store:** Tap the "App Store" icon on your home screen to open it.

4. **Search for Apps:** Use the search bar at the bottom to find the app you want. You can search by app name, category, or keywords.

5. **App Details:** Tap on the app's icon to view its details, including a description, screenshots, user reviews, and ratings.

6. **Download the App:** If the app is free, tap "Get" button to start the download. If it's a paid app, tap the price button then confirm the purchase with your Apple ID password or Face ID/Touch ID.

7. **Wait for Download:** App will begin downloading, and you'll spot its icon on your home screen. You can keep an eye on the download's progress through the app's icon.

Organizing Apps:

1. **Home Screen:** Your home screen is where you'll find your most frequently used apps. You can organize them by holding down an app icon until all icons start wiggling.

2. **Rearrange Icons:** While the icons are wiggling, drag an app icon to a new location on the home screen. You can also create app folders by dragging one app icon onto another. Give the folder a name and add more apps to it.

3. **Delete Apps:** To delete an app, tap the "x" icon in the corner of the app's icon while the icons are wiggling. Deleting an app will remove it from your device but not your App Store purchase history.

4. **App Library:** Swipe left to access your App Library, where apps are automatically categorized into groups like "Recently Added," "Social," and "Entertainment." You can search for apps using search bar at the top or browse through categories.

5. **Search for Apps:** To find a specific app, swipe down on the home screen or App Library to reveal the search bar. Type the app's name, and the search results will appear.

6. **Organize in Folders:** You can create folders in the App Library by dragging one app icon onto another. This is an excellent way to keep your apps organized without cluttering your home screen.

7. **Offload Unused Apps:** To save storage space, you can enable the "Offload Unused Apps" feature in "Settings" > "App Store." This will automatically remove apps that you rarely use but keep their data, allowing you to reinstall them when needed.

Health, Communication, and Leisure App for Seniors

As a senior with an iPhone 15, you have a world of apps at your fingertips to enhance your daily life and well-being. From staying connected with loved ones to managing your health and enjoying leisure activities, there's an app for nearly every aspect of senior living. In this section, we'll explore essential apps in three key categories: health, communication, and leisure, designed to improve your quality of life and provide valuable resources.

Health and Wellness Apps:

1. **MyFitnessPal:** Maintaining a healthy lifestyle is crucial for seniors. MyFitnessPal is a versatile app that helps you track your diet, exercise, and weight. It offers a vast database of foods & exercises, making it easy to monitor your nutrition and fitness goals.

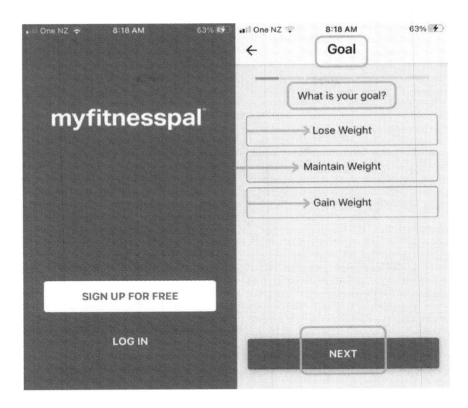

2. **Medisafe:** Managing medications can be challenging, especially when multiple prescriptions are involved. Medisafe is a medication reminder app that helps you take your pills on time and stay organized with your medication schedule.

3. **Heart Rate Monitor:** Keeping an eye on your heart rate is vital for heart health. Many apps, such as HeartWatch and Cardiogram, can track your heart rate using your iPhone's built-in sensors, providing valuable insights into your cardiovascular health.

4. **AARP Now:** The AARP Now app offers resources and information relevant to seniors. It provides access to articles, news, events, and member benefits from the American Association of Retired Persons (AARP).

Communication and Connection Apps:

1. **WhatsApp:** Staying in touch with family and friends is easier than ever with WhatsApp. This free messaging app lets you to send text messages, make voice

& video calls, and share photos and videos with loved ones, even if they're in different parts of the world.

2. **Skype:** Skype is another excellent app for making video calls and staying connected with family and friends. It's user-friendly and supports group video calls, making it an ideal choice for keeping in touch with multiple people at once.

3. **Facebook:** Facebook is a versatile platform for connecting with people & staying updated on the latest news, events, and trends. The app allows you to engage with family and friends through posts, comments, and messages.

4. **Zoom:** This is a popular video conferencing app that has become increasingly important for remote communication. It's useful for virtual family gatherings, staying connected with support groups, and participating in online classes.

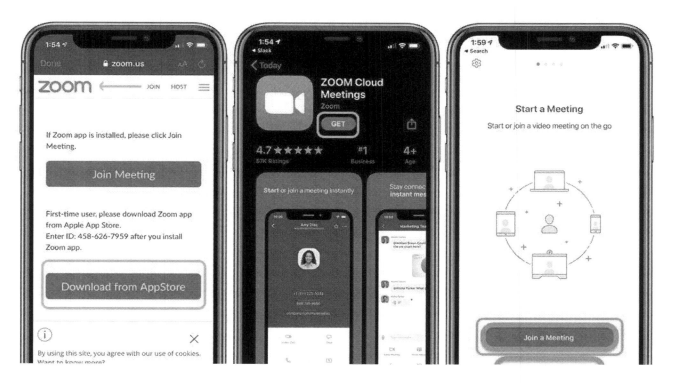

Leisure and Entertainment Apps:

1. **Audible:** Reading is a beloved pastime, and Audible takes it to the next level by offering a vast library of audiobooks. Whether you're relaxing at home or on the go, you can listen to your favorite books narrated by professional voice actors.

2. **Kindle:** The Kindle app is perfect for seniors who love to read. It allows you to purchase and read e-books on your iPhone. You can adjust text size, font, and background color for a personalized reading experience.

3. **Calm:** Calm is an app specifically created for meditation and relaxation, aimed at reducing stress and enhancing mental well-being. It offers guided meditation sessions, soothing music, and sleep stories to help you unwind & improve your sleep quality.

4. **Spotify:** Music can be a source of joy and relaxation. Using Spotify, you can enjoy a vast music library, personalized playlists, and the option to curate your music collections. It's a platform for listening to your favorite songs and exploring new tracks.

5. **Lumosity:** Lumosity is an app dedicated to brain training, featuring an assortment of enjoyable and challenging games tailored to enhance memory, attention, and problem-solving skills. Engaging with these games can help keep your mind sharp and active.

Chapter 9:
Advanced Features and Customization

Customizing Your iPhone Experience

T he iPhone 15 Pro and 15 Pro Max have new Super Retina XDR displays that are fluid and high-quality. It is such a nice display and is aesthetically pleasing. There are several ways you can customize your display to make the most of your new Pro iPhone.

Appearance

- To customize your display, just go to **Settings**, and then go down to "**Display & Brightness**." You're going to see tons of customizable options.

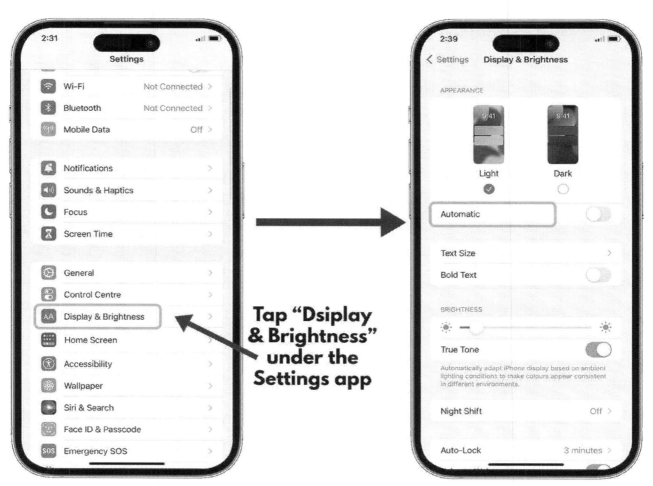

Tap "Dsiplay & Brightness" under the Settings app

First is the "**Appearance**" section. You have the option between "**Light**" and "**Dark**" mode for how your iPhone appears. By default, your iPhone is in "**Light**," but if we want to make it dark, select "**Dark**" from the Appearance segment, and your iPhone will turn all the background pixels on your phone black while the overlaying text will be white.

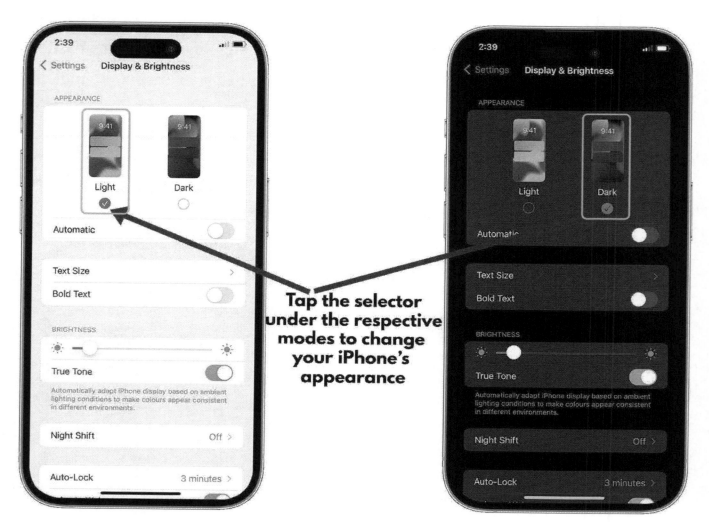

Tap the selector under the respective modes to change your iPhone's appearance

Underneath the "**Light**" and "**Dark**" modes is the "**Automatic**" tab. If you turn this on, it's going to give us a few options to go off of. So, essentially, by turning this on, you can have a scheduled time to change appearance automatically. So, if you want light mode on from "**Sunset to Sunrise**," it'll stay on during these time periods. As soon as the sun sets, your phone is going to transition into dark mode since it's now nighttime. You can also create your own custom schedule right here.

Text Size

Next is the "**Text Size**" tab. You can change the size of your text. The standard size is fine, but if you want it bigger because you have a hard time seeing the normal-sized text, you can always turn that up. If you want your text on your iPhone to be smaller, you can definitely do that as well.

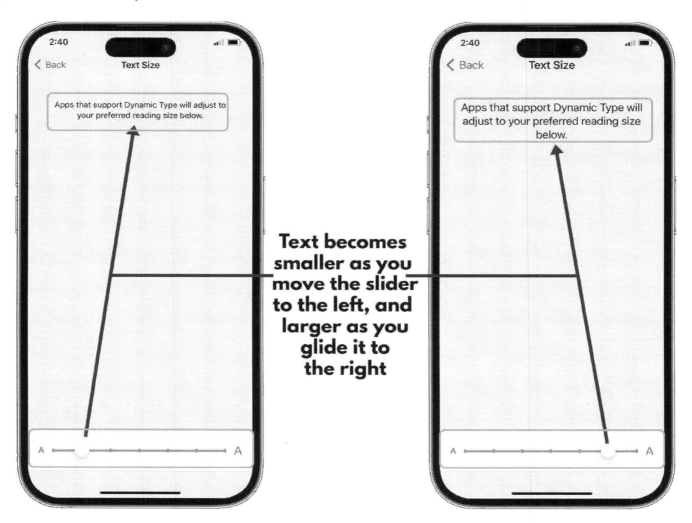

Bold Text

Next is the "**Bold Text**" toggle. If you turn on the "**Bold Text**" toggle, all the text on your screen is going to turn bold. This is completely up to you.

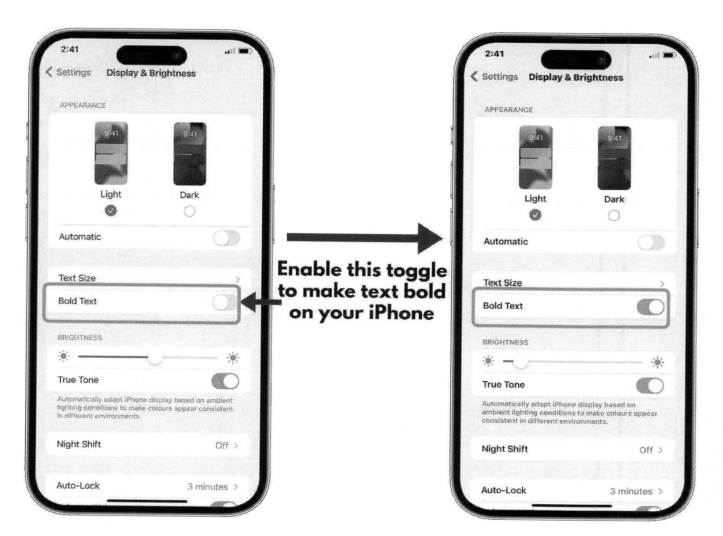

Brightness

You can use the "**Brightness**" slider below the "Text Size" tab to manually control your iPhone's brightness. There's also a slider in your iPhone's Control Center for manual brightness control.

True Tone

Below the "Brightness" slider is **True Tone**. True Tone uses a number of sensors to automatically change the color temperature of your iPhone based on the light around you. This makes the display look more natural in different lighting conditions. It is recommended that you turn it on to get the most out of your iPhone's display.

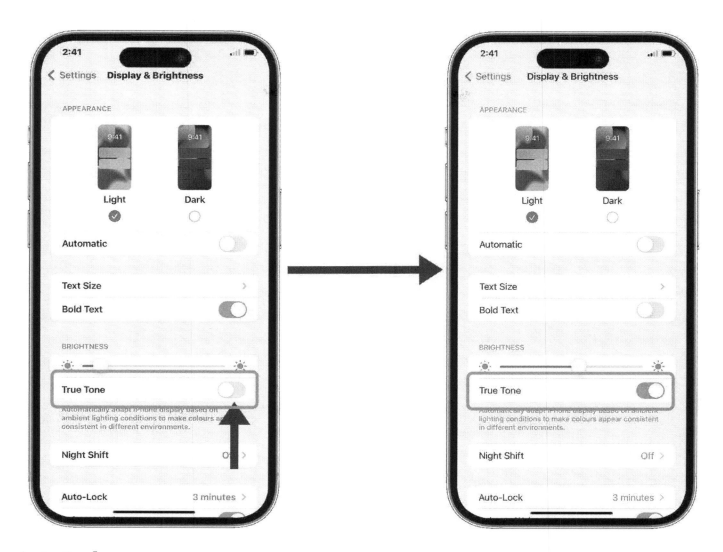

Auto-Lock

Another feature that you might find helpful is Auto-Lock, an iOS feature that determines how long your screen is going to stay unlocked before shutting off. When your iPhone senses that you're staring at the screen, it won't automatically lower the brightness. You can set your auto-lock to activate between 30 seconds and five minutes, or anywhere in between.

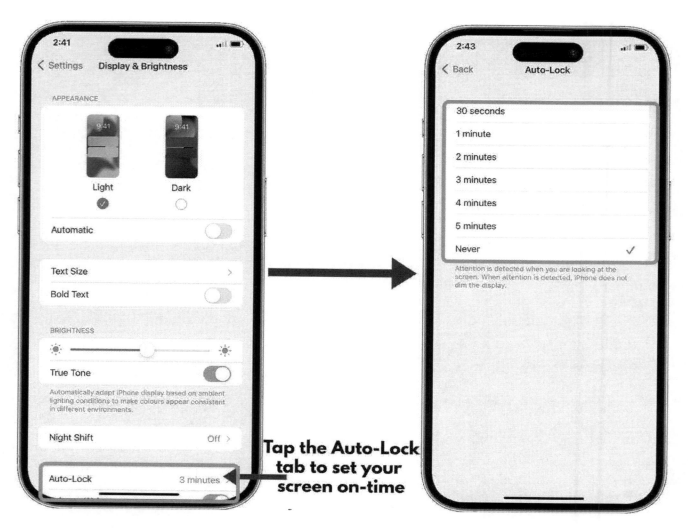

Tap the Auto-Lock tab to set your screen on-time

Always-On Display

A special feature for the iPhone 15 Pro or 15 Pro Max is the screen's Always-On Display. So, instead of your iPhone screen shutting off, with Always-On Display, the Lock Screen will dial down its brightness but remain viewable, so you can see any updates at any time without having to tap any buttons or touch the device. The screen is just going to be dimmer. And then, when you pick up your iPhone, it starts to get brighter and goes back to its normal display brightness. This is a feature on iPhone 15 Pro models.

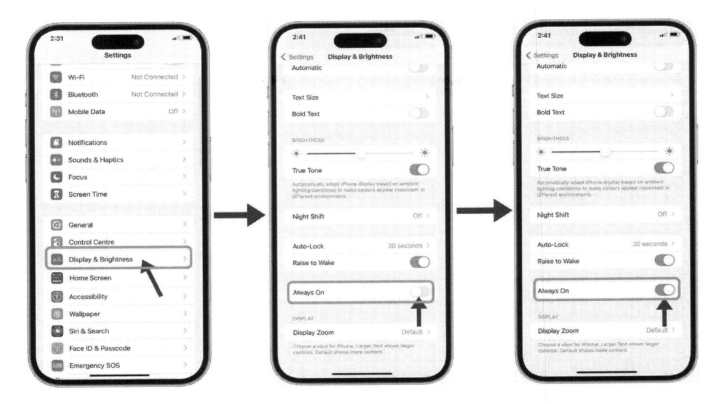

Nevertheless, keep in mind that when it's in your pocket or lying face-down, the screen will go black so that your device can save battery life. This is a great feature for the iPhone 15 Pro Model.

How to add and edit widgets on your iPhone's Home Screen

As you might be aware, if you have an iPhone, you can add widgets to your Home Screen. If you touch and hold on any empty portion of the Home Screen, the apps will start jiggling. You'll find a plus (+) button at the top-right corner of the screen.

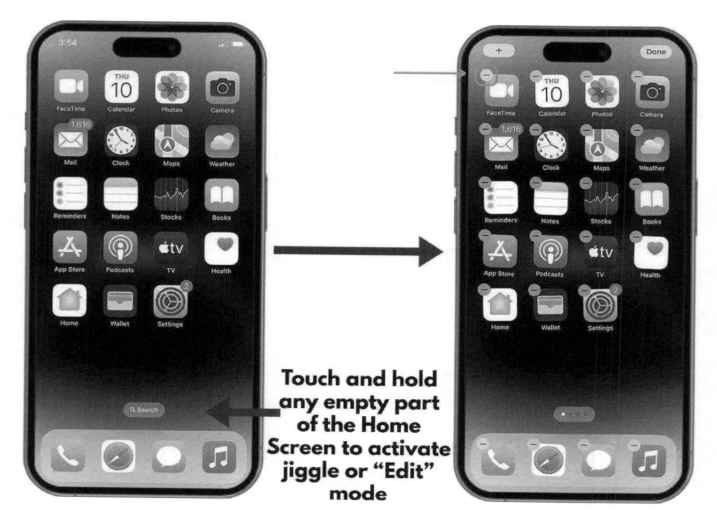

Touch and hold any empty part of the Home Screen to activate jiggle or "Edit" mode

To add a widget, tap that plus (+) button. This will reveal the widget library, where you'll have access to several widgets you can choose from, ranging anywhere from Notes, Reminders, Fitness, News, Photos, and anything else you want.

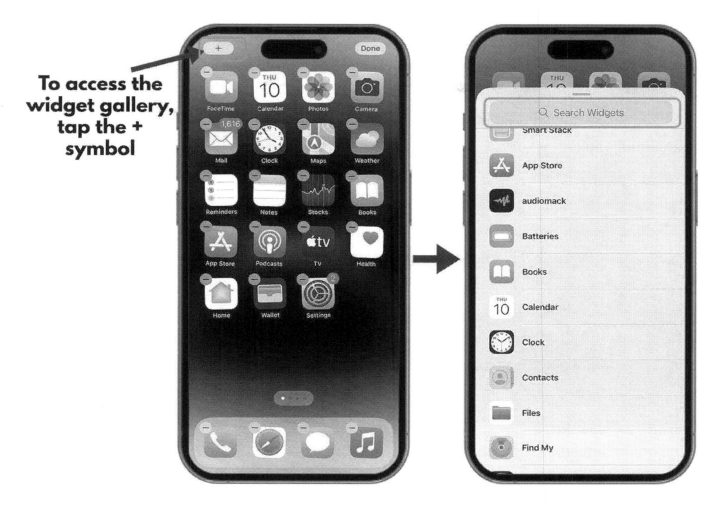

To access the widget gallery, tap the + symbol

Essentially, you can choose and add any of the above-mentioned widgets (and more) to your Home Screen. So, for example, if you want to add a widget for your battery to your Home Screen, you can do it directly from the widget gallery. Tapping on any of the provided widget options will show the three standard sizes available to choose from. The small widget has a square icon. The medium-sized widget is rectangular in shape, and the final size is often the large one.

Tap any widget you wish to add to your iPhone's Home Screen. Let's use the Calendar widget as an example

Immediately after you tap the "**Add Widget**" button below the size you want, your iPhone adds it to your Home Screen.

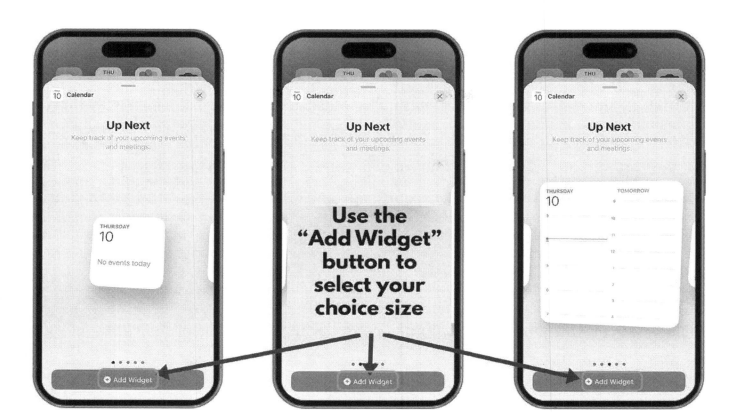

Use the "Add Widget" button to select your choice size

After you've made all edits, tap "Done" to save

Using iCloud and Other Apple Services

iCloud serves as Apple's secure cloud-based storage for your music, photos, videos, documents, and more. This allows seamless access to your information across all your devices, and in case of loss or theft, iCloud can aid in locating your device. Wondering why you should utilize iCloud for your iPhone 15? It provides a straightforward method to safeguard crucial pictures, contacts, and documents, especially considering the statistics—Asurion's 2021 claims data indicates that over 46 million phones are lost, stolen, or damaged annually. Therefore, having a backup plan is essential.

An additional benefit is that when upgrading to a new phone, iCloud simplifies the transfer of everything from your old device to the new one. To set up iCloud on your iPhone 15, follow these steps:

Setting up iCloud on iPhone or iPad

1. Navigate to Settings > [Your name] > iCloud.

2. Enter your Apple ID and password.

3. Turn on the desired features.

Setting up iCloud on Mac Computer

1. Go to the Apple Menu (top-left icon).

2. Click on System Preferences then Apple ID and select iCloud.

3. Enter your Apple ID & password, then activate the desired features.

For backing up your iPhone to iCloud, ensure you are connected to Wi-Fi and that your software is updated. Follow these steps:

1. Go to Settings then [Your name] then iCloud.

2. Tap the iCloud Backup then Back Up Now.

3. Stay connected to Wi-Fi 'til the backup is complete. If storage is insufficient, manage it through iCloud > Manage Storage.

To enable automatic backups:

1. Tap Settings > [Your name] > iCloud.

2. Toggle on/off each item for automatic backup.

To transfer data to a new phone using iCloud:

1. Follow the backup instructions.

2. During setup on the new device, choose Restore from iCloud Backup, sign in, then select the desired backup.

To set up iCloud Photos and manage storage:

1. Turn on Photos in your settings, and if storage is an issue, choose Optimize iPhone Storage.

For restoring iOS devices from an iCloud backup:

1. Ensure the device has the latest software update.

2. Check the last backup date in Settings > [Your name] > iCloud > iCloud Backup.

3. Go to Settings then General > Transfer or Reset iPhone, tap Erase All Content and Settings.

4. On the Apps & Data screen, choose Restore from iCloud Backup, sign in, and select the desired backup.

Advanced Tips for Experienced Users

Experience a multitude of innovative features with the iPhone 15 Pro, thanks to enhanced hardware and software upgrades. This compilation highlights fifteen features, many of which are compatible with the iPhone 15 and older models running iOS 17. Some of these features are beloved classics that are essential to explore.

1. Music Recognition with the Action Button (15 Pro/15 Pro Max Only)

The Action Button on the iPhone 15 Pro, replacing the mute switch, serves various functions, including activating the torch, recording voice memos, and launching the camera. Utilize Siri Shortcuts, such as Shazam integration, by pressing and holding the button to recognize nearby music.

2. Efficient App Folder Management

Easily drag multiple apps into a folder simultaneously by tapping and holding one app icon, then selecting others before dragging the entire collection into an existing folder.

3. Battery Optimization (Charge up to 80%)

Enhance battery longevity by setting a charging limit of 80%. Access this feature in Settings > Battery > Battery Health and Charging > Charging Optimization.

4. Rain Sounds with a Button Press

Generate soothing rain sounds with a triple click of the side button by configuring the feature in Settings > Accessibility > Audio/Vision > Background Sounds.

5. Text Capture and Translation with the Camera

Capture and translate text using the camera by tapping the text icon that appears when the phone detects text. Choose from options like copy, select, look up, translate, and share.

6. Effortless Photo Cropping

Crop photos easily by opening the image in the Photos app, pinching to zoom until the desired size is achieved, and tapping 'Crop' in the top right corner.

7. Custom Sticker Creation from Photos

Create custom stickers in the Photos app by selecting a photo, separating the subject from the background, and tapping 'add sticker' from the pop-up menu.

8. Offline Apple Maps Download

Download select areas for offline navigation in Apple Maps by accessing Maps > profile image > offline maps > download new map.

9. Visual Look Up for Laundry Care Icons

Use Visual Look Up in iOS 17 to understand laundry care icons by taking a photo of a label, tapping the 'i' icon, and selecting Visual Look Up.

10. Apple Logo as a Secret Button

Enable the back tap feature to take screenshots or launch functions by tapping near the Apple logo. Configure in Settings > Accessibility > Touch > Back Tap.

11. Multiple Timers with Labels

Run multiple timers with different labels by accessing the Clock app, setting timers, and tapping the '+' icon to add more.

12. Copy and Paste Photo Edits

Copy & paste edits from one photo to apply them to multiple shots by editing an image, copying edits, and pasting them to selected photos.

13. Shoot in LOG (15 Pro/15 Pro Max Only)

Explore shooting in Log mode on the iPhone 15 Pro for enhanced color data. Enable in Settings > Camera > Formats > ProRes Encoding.

14. Different Focal Length for Primary Camera

Choose a default focal length for the primary camera other than the default 24mm wide. Adjust in Settings > Camera > Main Camera.

15. Keyboard Trackpad Feature

Use the built-in trackpad feature on the iPhone keyboard by pressing and holding the space bar to navigate the cursor precisely while typing.

Chapter 10:

Troubleshooting and Security

Solving Basic Problems and Where to Get Help

Presented below are the six most common issues encountered with the iPhone 15, along with effective solutions to resolve them:

1. **iPhone 15 Activation Troubles**

If you're facing challenges activating your new iPhone 15, this is a common issue, especially during the initial days of the iPhone's release. Possible reasons include heavy traffic on Apple servers or connectivity issues with your cellular network or Wi-Fi. Patience is key, as it could be due to high server demand.

2. **iPhone 15 Fails to Power On**

In some instances, even a fresh iPhone 15 may not power on. This could be attributed to a depleted battery. Ensure you charge the device adequately and attempt to power it on again. If unsuccessful, a minor software glitch might be the cause, and a hard reset could be the solution.

3. **Rapid Battery Drain on iPhone 15**

If your iPhone 15's battery is depleting quickly, outdated iOS software might be the culprit. Check for and install the latest updates in the settings. Additionally, scrutinize your app usage patterns and background processes, identifying and closing power-hungry apps. Disable Bluetooth, location services, Wi-Fi, and cellular data when not in use to conserve battery life.

4. **iPhone 15 (Pro Max) Overheating**

Overheating issues can arise during resource-intensive tasks like gaming or video calls. Closing such applications and allowing the device to cool down can alleviate this. External factors like hot environments or using a back case can also contribute to overheating. Ensure proper ventilation to dissipate heat effectively.

5. **iPhone 15 Refuses to Charge**

When your iPhone 15 isn't charging, inspect your charging cable and adapter, ensuring they are Apple-certified. Changing the cable and adapter, as well as cleaning the charging port from debris, can resolve charging issues. Use a soft material like a cotton bud or compressed air for cleaning.

6. **iPhone 15 Camera Malfunctions**

Camera problems on the iPhone 15 may stem from software glitches. If the camera app won't open, close it from recent apps or restart your iPhone. Updating to the latest iOS version is advisable. If issues persist, consider resetting all settings in Settings >> General >> Transfer & Reset iPhone >> Reset All Settings.

Keeping Your iPhone Secure and Updated

Automatically Update iPhone's iOS

Turn on automatic updates with the steps below:

1. In Settings app on your iPhone ⚙, click **General.**

2. Select **Software Update** & click **Automatic Updates.**

3. Then switch on '**Download iOS Updates**' & '**Install iOS Updates.**'

When you switch on this option, the iPhone will search for and install new updates at night when your device is charging & connected to Wi-Fi.

Force Restart the iPhone

At times, you would notice that the iPhone isn't responding to touch. Force restart would solve whatever is causing this.

1. Press and immediately release the button that controls the volume up, then press and fast release the button that controls the volume down, and finally, press and hold the side button until the Apple logo appears.

2. Release the button once the logo appears.

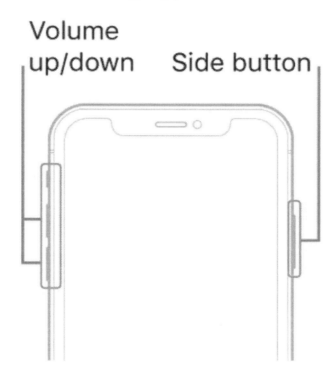

Manually Update iPhone's iOS

1. In Settings app on your iPhone ⚙, click **General.**

2. Select **Software Update** to check for any new updates.

3. Click any available update to download & install it.

Back Up your iPhone 15 Using Windows PC

1. Connect your computer & your iPhone 15 with a cable.

2. Install & open the iTunes app, then tap the iPhone 15 tab close to the upper left side of the iTunes window.

3. Click **Summary** & select **Back Up Now.**

Back up your iPhone 15 Using Mac

1. Connect your Mac & your iPhone 15 with a cable.

2. Open the Finder sidebar on your Mac & click your iPhone 15

3. Click **General** at the top of that screen, then choose **"Back up all of the data on your iPhone 15 to this Mac."**

4. Then select **'Back Up Now.'**

Return iPhone 15 Settings to Default

Return all iPhone 15 settings to their default state without losing your content. Although this shouldn't affect your content, I would still recommend that you back up your iPhone 15 before you do these steps.

1. In Settings app on your iPhone 🔘, click **General.**

2. Select **Transfer or Reset iPhone 15** & click **Reset.**

3. Now choose an option:

   o **Reset All Settings** – return all your settings to their default, including location & privacy, network settings, & more. Your media & data remain.

   o **Reset Network Settings** – remove all network settings changes, including changes done to the device name.

   o **Reset Keyboard Dictionary** – new words are automatically added to the Keyboard dictionary when you reject the iPhone's suggestions as you type. This option will delete all the new additions.

   o **Reset Home Screen Layout** – changes the home screen layout to its default & discards every change you made.

   o **Reset Location & Privacy** – reverses all changes you made to your privacy settings & location services.

Erase iPhone

Warning: this step will wipe off everything you have on your iPhone 15. Most people perform this step when they want to sell or give away their device.

1. In Settings app on your iPhone ⚙, click **General.**

2. Select **Transfer or Reset iPhone 15** & click **Erase All Content & Settings.**

Erase Your iPhone 15 Using a Computer

You can also wipe off the iPhone 15 using your computer. Remember that this will completely remove every setting and content on your device.

1. Connect your Mac or PC & your iPhone 15 with a cable.

2. On your Mac, do the following:

   o Open the Finder sidebar on your Mac & click your iPhone, then click **General** & click **Restore iPhone 15**

3. On your Windows PC, do the following:

   o Open the iTunes app, tap the iPhone 15 tab close to the upper left side of the window, click **Summary,** & click **Restore iPhone**
   o Continue with the onscreen instructions.

Restore iPhone 15 from a Computer Backup

1. Connect your Mac or PC & your iPhone 15 with a cable.

2. On your Mac, do the following:

   o Open the Finder sidebar on your Mac & click your iPhone, then click **Trust**.

3. On your Windows PC, do the following:

   o Open the iTunes app, tap the device tab close to the upper left side of the window & select your iPhone 15

4. On the welcome screen, select **"Restore from this backup,"** tap the right backup & click **Continue.**

Privacy and Data Management

The iPhone is engineered to safeguard both your data and privacy. Its built-in privacy features are designed to limit access to your information, ensuring that you have control over what is shared and where. Security features are also embedded to prevent unauthorized access to your iPhone and iCloud data. To maximize the effectiveness of these privacy and security features, follow these recommended practices:

Protect Access to Your iPhone

1. **Set a strong passcode:** Establishing a robust passcode is crucial for safeguarding your device.

2. **Use Face ID:** Employ the secure and convenient Face ID or Touch ID for unlocking your iPhone, authorizing purchases, and signing into third-party apps.

3. **Turn on Find My iPhone:** Activate Find My to locate your iPhone if lost or stolen, and to prevent unauthorized use.

Keep Your Apple ID Secure: Your Apple ID grants access to your iCloud data and account information for services like the App Store & Apple Music. Ensure its security by following guidelines outlined in "Keep your Apple ID secure on iPhone."

Make Account Sign-ins Safer and Easier

1. **Sign in with passkeys:** Use Face ID or Touch ID for sign-ins, eliminating the need for passwords.

2. **Use Sign in with Apple:** Utilize your Apple ID for sign-ins, benefiting from two-factor authentication and limited information sharing.

3. **Let iPhone create strong passwords:** Allow iPhone to generate strong passwords automatically for services lacking passkey or Sign in with Apple support.

Manage Information Sharing

1. **Use Safety Check:** Conveniently review and update shared information and immediately halt sharing if personal safety is at risk.

2. **Control app tracking:** Manage app permissions for tracking and modify them later if needed.

3. **Control what you share with apps:** Review and adjust data sharing preferences with apps, location information, hardware information, and advertising delivery settings.

4. **Review privacy practices:** Check the App Privacy Report and developer-reported summary in the App Store for app privacy practices.

Protect Email Privacy

1. **Turn on Mail Privacy Protection:** Enhance the security of your Mail activity by hiding your IP address.

2. **Use Hide My Email:** Generate unique, random email addresses with iCloud+ to protect your personal email address.

Secure Web Browsing

1. **Use iCloud Private Relay:** Subscribers to iCloud+ can enhance online privacy by preventing detailed profiling by websites and network providers.

2. **Manage privacy in Safari:** Review the Privacy Report, adjust Safari settings, and prevent trackers from following your online activities.

Lock Down Your iPhone in Sophisticated Cyberattacks: In case of sophisticated remote attacks, use Lockdown Mode for an extreme level of security. This feature automatically protects Safari, Messages, Home, and various Apple services and apps, though it may result in reduced performance and usability during operation.

Chapter 11:
Conclusion and Resources

Embracing Technology at Any Age

Embracing technology, especially for seniors, holds transformative potential, exemplified by the iPhone 15. Despite initial apprehensions, seniors can derive immense benefits from this advanced device. The user-friendly interface, intuitive design, and accessibility features cater to diverse needs, making it an ideal companion for individuals of any age.

The iPhone 15 fosters connectivity, enabling seniors to stay in touch with loved ones through video calls, messaging, and social media. Its health and fitness apps empower users to monitor and manage their well-being effortlessly. The device's robust camera captures cherished moments, turning it into a tool for preserving memories.

Furthermore, the iPhone 15's voice command capabilities and AI-driven assistance simplify tasks, making technology more inclusive and less intimidating for seniors. Embracing such advancements can enhance cognitive abilities, promote mental stimulation, and combat feelings of isolation.

As society becomes increasingly digital, seniors who embrace technology open avenues for lifelong learning and engagement. The iPhone 15 serves as a gateway to information, entertainment, and cultural enrichment, ensuring that seniors remain active participants in the ever-evolving digital landscape.

The iPhone 15's features make it an invaluable asset for seniors, fostering a sense of empowerment, connection, and adaptability. Embracing technology at any age is not just a choice but a key to unlocking a world of possibilities, enriching the lives of seniors and bridging generational gaps in our tech-driven society.

Continuing Your iPhone Journey

Continuing your iPhone journey as a senior involves ongoing exploration and utilization of the device's features to enhance various aspects of your life. Delving into additional functionalities can significantly enrich your experience and make the most of this advanced technology.

Firstly, consider leveraging the accessibility features tailored for seniors. Explore settings such as larger text, bold fonts, and voiceover functions to customize the iPhone interface according to your preferences and needs. The device's commitment to inclusivity ensures a seamless and enjoyable user experience for everyone.

As you continue your iPhone journey, delve into the world of applications. The App Store offers a plethora of options catering to diverse interests. Whether it's reading, gaming, or accessing educational content, there's an app for virtually every interest. Engaging with these apps not only provides entertainment but also fosters ongoing learning and mental stimulation.

Stay connected with family & friends through social media platforms. Embrace the power of digital communication to share experiences, photos, and updates. Video calls and messaging apps can bridge geographical gaps, fostering a sense of closeness with loved ones.

Moreover, explore the iPhone's organizational tools. Utilize calendars, reminders, and note-taking apps to stay on top of appointments, birthdays, and other important events. These features can enhance your daily routine and contribute to a more organized & efficient lifestyle.

Lastly, stay informed about updates and new features introduced by Apple. Regularly checking for software updates ensures that your device remains secure, and you can benefit from the latest enhancements and improvements.

In essence, continuing your iPhone journey involves an ongoing commitment to learning, exploring, and integrating technology into your daily life. By embracing the device's full potential, you can enjoy a more connected, informed, and enriched lifestyle as a senior in the digital age.

Glossary of Terms

AirDrop: Transmit files wirelessly between Apple devices such as iPhone and Mac.

Airplane Mode: Used to deactivate the internet connection during flights. Also useful for turning off Wi-Fi connections.

AirPlay: Establishes a wireless connection between an iPhone and a TV or other display devices.

AirPrint: Enables wireless printing of documents.

Animoji: Animated emojis created using facial expressions captured by the iPhone camera.

App Switcher: Allows viewing of apps running in the background and selecting the desired app.

Apple ID: refers to the Apple account that is required in order to log into the App Store or iTunes in order to purchase applications.

Apple Pay: Apple's online payment system.

Assistive Touch: is a soft button that is presented on the screen for the goal of making the device more accessible. Options that can be customized including the home button, notifications, Siri, and other features. Proceed to 'Settings > General > Accessibility' to activate the feature.

Bluetooth: Using Bluetooth, your iPhone can establish a wireless connection to a different Bluetooth-enabled device that is located near it.

Bookmark: The bookmarking feature in Safari allows users to save webpages for later use.

Camera Roll: All of the photographs that were shot with the iPhone camera are stored in the Camera Roll.

Cellular: It refers to the availability of cellular network service when a SIM card is used for calling and browsing. Adjust the settings by going to the "Settings > Cellular" menu.

Control Center: A collection of shortcuts comprised of the Control Center. To access the control center, swipe up from the bottom of the screen in the upward direction.

Cover Sheet: You can access the Cover Sheet by swiping down from the top of the screen. It shows each of the alerts.

Digital Touch: The Messages app allows you to transmit handwritten or drawn sketches as well as messages whenever you use Digital Touch. When the video is being recorded, it is also accessible.

Do Not Disturb: Settings that allow you to block notifications and calls are referred to as "Do Not Disturb." To receive calls exclusively from preferred callers, this feature can be customized.

Emergency SOS: Using the iPhone, you can make calls to emergency contacts using the Emergency SOS feature.

Emoji: Emoticons and smileys that may be included in chats and documents are referred to as emojis. The iOS keyboard allows users to put emojis or animojis into their messages.

FaceTime: A video and audio calling application that can accommodate up to 32 users on a single call is known as FaceTime.

Family Sharing: Up to six members of the family are able to share purchases made from the App Store, iTunes, and Books store using the Family Sharing feature.

Files: An application that allows you to manage all of the files and folders on your iPhone as well as cloud storage.

Find iPhone: There is an Apple software called Find iPhone that can assist you in locating all of your gadgets when they are connected to the internet.

Flyover: A 3D city tour feature in the Maps app.

Game Center: Stores all data related to games.

Guided Access: Guided Access is a feature that allows users to control the screen area of a specific application, which might help unlock a child's device. Accessibility can be activated by going to the Settings menu.

Handoff: In the event that multiple devices are linked to the same wireless network, you are able to keep working on documents throughout all of them.

HDR: It refers to the settings on a camera that enhance illumination.

Home: A Home app that assists in connecting all of the devices in your home that are enabled with HomeKit.

Home Screen: This screen, which displays all of the apps when you open the iPhone, is comparable to the desktop screen on a Mac.

HomeKit: It is a home automation system that functions by connecting various gadgets to the Home app.

iBooks: The iBooks app is a library that allows you to view all of the books that you have purchased from Apple.

iCloud: Storage in the cloud that allows for the synchronization of images, media data, and backups of iPhones. Invest in extra room for storage so that you may host more content.

iMovie: One of Apple's digital movie and video applications is called iMovie. Utilizing iMovie, you can create short videos.

iOS: Apple's mobile operating system for iPhone and iPad.

iTunes: Apple's music store for purchasing media content.

Keychain: On the iPhone and iPad, Apple's mobile operating system is referred to as iOS.

Keynote: It is a feature that stores passwords and enables users to access them on any device that is associated with the same Apple ID.

Location Services: It is a presentation program that is comparable to Microsoft PowerPoint in that it allows users to create slideshows and presentations.

Lock Screen: The screen visible when you wake the iPhone.

Low Power Mode: Location services enable applications to take advantage of your location in order to give individualized features. Enable by going to the "Settings > Privacy" menu.

Memories: The lock screen is the screen that appears when the iPhone is first turned on.

Messages: The messaging software on your iPhone that allows you to send text messages with animojis.

Notifications: Alerts from applications such as Messages, Facebook, and others include notifications. To see the notifications, swipe down from the top of the screen.

Numbers: An application that processes spreadsheets, similar to Microsoft Excel.

Pages: A word processing app like Microsoft Word.

Panorama: A wide photo taken by moving the iPhone's camera.

Peek and Pop: A 3D Touch function that allows you to swiftly preview hyperlinks is called Peek and Pop. You can peep at the content by pressing, and you can pop it by pressing even harder.

Personal Hotspot: This feature enables you to share the cellular connection of your iPhone with many other devices.

Podcasts: An application developed by Apple that allows users to search for and subscribe to audio and video podcasts.

QR Code: A Quick Response (QR) code is a barcode that can be read by machines and that the camera of an iPhone can read to follow an activity.

Safari: The default web browser for iPhone and Mac.

Settings: On your iPhone, you will find an application called Settings that contains all of the customization choices for iOS. Because it is a default application, it cannot be removed.

Signature: Your signature is an email signature that is applied to every one of the emails that you send from your iPhone.

Siri: Siri is the voice assistant developed by Apple that allows users to conduct searches and a variety of other tasks by using voice commands.

Touch ID: Fingerprint unlocking through the Home button.

Trackpad: In the context of actions that are traditionally performed with a mouse, a trackpad is a finger trace pad.

VPN: A Virtual Private Network connection, indicated by an icon in the top menu bar.

Wallet: Apple's Wallet is an application that allows users to save credit card information for use in Apple Pay transactions.

Wallpaper: An image that serves as a background and is displayed on the home screen and the lock screen. Through the 'Settings > background' menu, you can give your home screen and lock screen a new background.

Wi-Fi: A wireless network connection.

Made in the USA
Columbia, SC
20 May 2024